The I

CW00410134

Also by Georgina Lloyd and published by Bantam Books

One Was Not Enough
Motive to Murder
The Evil that Men Do
With Malice Aforethought

The Passion Killers

Fifteen Murders in Hot Blood

GEORGINA LLOYD

BANTAM BOOKS
TORONTO · NEW YORK · LONDON · SYDNEY · AUCKLAND

THE PASSION KILLERS
A BANTAM BOOK 0 553 40422 9

Originally published in Great Britain by Robert Hale Ltd

PRINTING HISTORY
Robert Hale edition published 1990
Bantam edition published 1992

This book is set in Palatino

Bantam Books are published by Transworld Publishers Ltd.,
61–63 Uxbridge Road, Ealing, London W5 5SA, in Australia by
Transworld Publishers (Australia) Pty. Ltd., 15–23 Helles Avenue,
Moorebank, NSW 2170, and in New Zealand by Transworld
Publishers (N.Z.) Ltd., Cnr. Moselle and Waipareira Avenues,
Henderson, Auckland.

Printed and bound in Great Britain by
Cox & Wyman Ltd., Reading, Berks.

Contents

Introduction 7

1 **Paris Green**
William Waite (1969) 9

2 **A Constable named Sherlock**
The Red Mini Murder (1967) 20

3 **Passion vs. Promotion**
James Ronald Robertson (1950) 33

4 **Take a Letter, Miss Smith**
Madeleine Smith (1857) 41

5 **The Triangle of Death**
Edith Thompson and Frederick Bywaters (1922) 68

6 **The Cyclops Eye**
Dr Buck Ruxton (1935) 82

7 **Passion at the Villa Madeira**
Alma Rattenbury and George Stoner (1935) 100

8 **Tinker, Taylor, Soldier . . .**
Marcus Marymont (1958) 113

9 **The Suicide that Wasn't**
Frederick Emmett-Dunne (1953) 119

10 **A Deadly Bedside Manner**
Dr Hawley Harvey Crippen (1910) 127

11 **For Love of a Gipsy**
Charlotte Bryant (1935) 140

12 **The Fatal Blow**
Bertie Manton (1942) 148

13 **The Chalkpit Murder**
Thomas Ley and Lawrence Smith (1946)   157

14 **Dear John . . .**
Leslie George Stone (1936)   171

15 **The Wigwam Girl**
August Sangret (1942)   178

Introduction

The killing of a wife, mistress, husband or lover, or of a rival in love, is, if the statistics are anything to go by, the second commonest type of murder. Only murder for gain holds sway in the top group of figures. Like killing for gain, this motive is comparatively easy for the average person to understand. Love – imagined or real – or infatuation runs the gamut of our all too human emotions.

There is the calf-love of inexperienced teenagers, overwhelmed by the burgeoning of their sexual feelings, who imagine that the good-looking boy next door or that gorgeous blonde in the classroom is the great love of their life. At the other end of the scale we have the desperation of the middle-aged man who feels that life is rapidly passing him by, or the fortyish woman whose approaching menopause does nothing for her confidence and femininity. Both will clutch at the straws of what may prove to be only a transitory happiness, although in a few cases it can and does last. Somewhere in the middle are the men and women in their twenties and thirties who suffer all the throes of unrequited love, physical passion and that green-eyed monster, jealousy.

Murder, however, is no solution to any of these problems. Divorce is one answer, but sometimes the married partners cannot or will not divorce, and the lovelorn protagonists in the drama have very few other options open to them. They can wait it out, or they can leave home and elope to start a new life elsewhere, albeit without benefit of wedlock. Another option is to try resolutely to banish the feelings of love for the unattainable object of their desire and return to the bosom of the family – a tall order frequently found to be impossible. This course of action is the one mainly chosen when children are involved – 'We decided to stay together for the sake of the children' has a familiar, as well as familial, ring.

This book describes fifteen cases in which none of the above options was considered feasible by the participants, who unwisely decided that the simplest course of action was to poison, shoot, stab or strangle the unfaithful spouse, the rival in love, or the partner who stood in the way of whatever brand of happiness they were pursuing. Neither the threat of the hangman nor the fear of a lifetime in prison deterred them, though it may well, perhaps, have deterred a few others who might have been tempted to follow their example.

They gambled all for love – and they lost.

Georgina Lloyd
July 1989

1

Paris Green

William Waite (1969)

No one who knew William Waite and his wife Beryl would ever have thought them to be anything but an average happily married couple. Theirs had been a conventional courtship: Waite, an ex-soldier in the Royal Tank Regiment, met Beryl Waldon at a Services' social and dance, an event which had been kept up after the cessation of hostilities, in the autumn of 1949, and three years later they had married. In that same year Waite, whose father had been batman to Lord Leigh during the war, obtained a post at Stoneleigh Abbey as personal chauffeur to Lord Leigh. The young couple were allotted the occupation of a flat on Lord Leigh's estate, and they had two children, Julia, followed two years later by William Robin.

Waite accompanied his employer on hunting and shooting trips to other parts of England and to Scotland, while Beryl was content to stay at home and look after the children, combined with a part-time job three days a week as a domestic help at the Abbey. Beryl was four years older than her husband.

For fourteen years the couple jogged along on the path of an easy and undemanding domesticity, seemingly contented with their lot. Then, in the summer of 1966, a young girl, Judith Regan, came to Stoneleigh Abbey to take up her first job as a typist in the estate office, straight from her Roman Catholic secondary school in Warwick. Just seventeen, she was attractively petite and dark-haired, and quiet and unassuming in manner. Up to that point she had led a sheltered life, having had no serious boyfriends – just the usual boy and girl friendships as part of a group. She was not one for gallivanting about, preferring to spend her spare time reading and sewing.

William Waite, who was frequently in the estate office during the course of his duties, noticed the quietly attractive new addition to the staff, but made no attempt to get to know her better until 1967, when a Christmas party, to which the staff was invited, was held by Jack Delaney, the head groom at Lord Leigh's stables. Waite and Judith Regan danced together several times, and when, towards the end of the festivities, someone turned out all the lights for a joke, Waite kissed her.

A few days after this he invited her to the New Year's Eve party he was holding at his own home. Still just nineteen, she was flattered and thrilled at being singled out by a man twice her age. At this party, too, someone turned all the lights out towards the end – and it is not beyond question that this time it had been arranged beforehand – who knows? Again Waite kissed Judith Regan under cover of the darkness that enveloped them.

Whether William Waite decided that this was a dangerous game he was playing which must be resisted, or whether the stolen kisses were unimportant to him – a simple party flirtation – is something no one can know for certain, although the latter explanation, in the light of later events, would seem to be somewhat unlikely. What is known, however, is that he did not make any attempt to contact Judith again for several weeks, nor is there any record that Judith had even mentioned him to anybody.

Then, towards the end of January 1968, Waite walked unexpectedly into Judith's office and asked her if she would go out with him that evening for a few drinks in a village pub. She agreed, and after the outing, before he took her home, he parked his red Volkswagen in a quiet country lane, where they kissed and cuddled in the back of his car.

Two weeks later the invitation was repeated, and on this occasion Judith surrendered her virginity to him in the back of his car. This was the beginning of a passionate clandestine affair, which was to increase in intensity throughout 1968 and into the spring and summer of 1969. They spent at least one evening together every week, after which occasional nights at hotels ensued, and whenever an opportunity occurred they would enjoy a weekend at a hotel, registering as 'Mr and Mrs White'.

About a year after their first outing, the lovers began to discuss the possibility of divorce for Waite, so that he could offer marriage to Judith. There was even talk of a honeymoon in Majorca to look forward to. Waite promised that he would tell his wife the truth and persuade her to divorce him, but actually he did not have the courage to carry out his intention and made no move towards this end. In fact, when his wife, who had heard rumours, asked him whether there was anything between him and the girl, he denied having any interest in her. Even his children were becoming suspicious. William junior found a handkerchief smelling of Judith's perfume in the car, and Julia, who was fourteen at the time, discovered a packet of contraceptives while she was cleaning the car; she knew, however, that her mother was on the pill.

Waite himself seems to have had problems of his own. At least, he told Dr Harold Parker, the family physician, in September 1968 that he was unable to have sexual intercourse with his wife, and when Dr Parker asked him whether there was any reason for this that he could think of, Waite replied, 'If you mean is there any other woman, there is no one else involved.' Waite was given a prescription, and when he later returned to the surgery for a further supply of the tablets, he told Dr Parker that he was 'much improved'.

While Waite was in Scotland with Lord Leigh in the autumn of 1968 he wrote loving letters to his wife, in which he referred to his inability to have intercourse with her. One of these letters included the words: 'I still love you with all my heart, strange as this may seem to you. I just cannot explain it, and I am trying so hard to think why this should be.' The letter was signed, 'Your dear loving husband, Bill.' Another letter read in part: 'I am praying that this will work out all right in the end. There must be something wrong with me. Leave the worry to me. Look after yourself . . . God bless you and keep you safe always.'

An intolerable pressure was beginning to build up in Waite's mind, and at one point he and Judith agreed that it

would be better to end their association. This break, however, was short-lived, because within three days Waite was
back in the estate office telling Judith that he could not live
without her. There is no evidence that Waite was ever less
than affectionate towards his wife, and it is impossible to
speculate as to why he eventually came to the decision that
murder rather than divorce was the answer to his problem.

Some time early in 1968 he began to introduce small
doses of 'Paris Green', an arsenic-based horticultural pesticide, into his wife's food and drink. On an estate such as
Stoneleigh Abbey there were, naturally, stocks of such
materials, so Waite had no need to arouse suspicion by
buying arsenical weedkiller or other poisonous substances.
Beryl Waite, normally a healthy and energetic woman,
began to grow thin and listless; she lost her appetite, and
could not sleep. In July 1968 she consulted Dr Parker, who
prescribed a tonic. She seemed to improve considerably,
but the doctor continued to see her at monthly intervals
until January 1969, when she had a severe bilious attack.
She then complained of swelling ankles, and numbness in
her hands and feet. Dr Parker was frankly puzzled by her
symptoms, and arranged for her to be admitted to Warne-
fort Hospital in Leamington Spa for observation. Her dis-
order was diagnosed as 'acute polyneuritis', believed to be
due to a virus or an allergy, and during her stay in hospital
her health improved a great deal.

After a month in hospital, Beryl Waite returned home in
April, seeming much better, but soon her old symptoms
returned, and she became a semi-invalid. Throughout
her illness her husband showed the greatest solicitude,
carrying her from one room to another when she felt well
enough to be moved; but she had completely lost the use of
her legs.

Judith Regan was a frequent visitor to the flat, helping
with the housework, doing the shopping, and sometimes
cooking meals for Waite and the two children. He and
Judith continued their weekly outings, usually on Satur-
days, when Waite would take drinks and glasses and they
would make love in the back of the car, the Volkswagen
having by this time been traded in for a silver-grey Cortina.

On Saturday, 6 September, they met as usual and spent about four hours together. On the following day Waite drove his employer to Hampshire, and on his return found his wife seriously ill. He sent for Dr Parker, who was not there at the time, so one of his partners, a Dr John Harger, came in response to the call and saw Mrs Waite. Her husband told Dr Harger that he thought his wife was suffering from gastro-enteritis. Dr Harger gave her an injection and left her a sleeping capsule, and told Waite that Dr Parker himself would call the next day. Waite gave the capsule to his wife in the presence of her sister, a Mrs Jones of Leamington Spa, who had been called because Mrs Waite was so ill. This capsule put Beryl Waite into a sleep from which she never awakened, her husband having previously emptied it and refilled it with arsenic. She died in the early hours of 8 September, weighing only 6½ stone.

Dr Harger issued a death certificate, but later that day he had second thoughts, since he was not entirely satisfied with some aspects of the illness that had preceded Mrs Waite's death. After first discussing the matter fully with Dr Parker, he contacted the Warwickshire coroner, Dr H. Tibbitts, who ordered a post-mortem. Mrs Waite's body was examined by Dr Derek Barrowcliff, a forensic pathologist, who found that it contained a thousand times more arsenic than could normally be found as a trace element in the body of a person who had died of natural causes. He concluded that a large dose of arsenic had been administered to Mrs Waite on the Friday before her death, followed by another similar dose on the Saturday, a massive dose on the Sunday morning and a final dose about six hours before her death. He thought that she had probably ingested a much larger quantity than he had actually found, since arsenic passes quite rapidly through the body. It was his considered opinion that the poison had been taken in regular doses since at least November 1968, or possibly even earlier.

Tests that Dr Barrowcliff made on hair samples pointed to an almost continuous administration of arsenic over a long period. One tellingly significant aspect of the tests was that one segment of the samples was free of arsenic; this

represented the period during which Mrs Waite had been
in hospital. Dr Barrowcliff made an experiment which he
was to describe later at the trial as 'not very scientific, but
successful'. The contamination of hair by sweat containing
arsenic sometimes affects the results of hair–arsenic analysis, but Dr Barrowcliff was able to prove that this could not
have occurred in the case of Mrs Waite, who was always
meticulously neat and well groomed, and even three days
before her death, although desperately ill, she had used
hair-spray in order to keep her coiffure tidy. Dr Barrowcliff
sprayed a piece of blotting-paper with the same kind of
lacquer that she had used, and when it had dried he wrote
on it with his fountain-pen. The lacquer stopped the water-
soluble ink from seeping through to the other side of the
blotting-paper as it would normally do, this proving that
perspiration could not have penetrated the sprayed hair to
leave a deposit of arsenic.

As soon as his wife's body had been removed by the
undertakers, Waite destroyed all the bedding and burned
other articles which she had used during her illness such as
towels, face flannel and so on. But he overlooked two
things: a packet of Paris Green pesticide in the eaves under
the roof of the estate garage where he worked; and, in a
cupboard at his home, an empty dispenser which had
contained anti-travel sickness pills and which, on analysis,
also revealed traces of Paris Green.

When Waite was first seen by detectives he made no
mention of his association with Judith Regan, but later
admitted that she was his mistress, adding that he would
have married her if he had been free. In reply to a suggestion that he thus had a motive for murdering his wife, he
replied, 'I did not kill her, if that's what you mean. I
couldn't do a thing like that.'

Six days after his wife's death, Waite attempted to kill
himself by swallowing a large quantity of aspirin tablets,
but he was found by one of his children, rushed to hospital
and recovered. At the time of his suicide attempt, he was
staying with his children at his parents' farm, and he left a
note addressed to them, in which he wrote: 'I didn't do it,
but I cannot stand all these questions . . . Please forgive me

for doing this to you all. I could not stop loving Judith. We did try so hard . . .'

William Waite was arrested and charged with the murder of his wife. When he stood in the dock at Birmingham Assizes, in February 1970, the prosecuting counsel, Mr Michael Davies, QC, said that Waite's motive was 'as old as the hills'. He was a married man who had fallen desperately in love with a young girl whom he wished to marry, but his wife had refused him a divorce, so she had to be removed from the scene. He was a man of previously unblemished character, and no one who knew him would ever have considered him likely to commit any kind of criminal offence, let alone murder. But from January 1968 until his wife's death he had been carrying on a secret association with Judith Regan, regularly having sexual intercourse with her; he had thus been living two separate lives, one with his wife and one with Miss Regan.

Referring to the events of the last weekend of Mrs Waite's life, Mr Davies said that it was true that Waite himself had called the doctor. 'You must give him credit for that,' he said, 'but you may feel that he was confident that he had fooled the doctors, as indeed he had up to the time of his wife's death.'

Judith Regan, who lived with her parents in St Michael's Road, Warwick, was called as a prosecution witness. She told the court how she kept a notebook with the dates of her meetings with William Waite. They went out together no fewer than sixty times between January 1968 and April 1969, after which date they made car trips about once a week. They had also stayed together as man and wife on at least three occasions. Mrs Waite had once asked her whether there was anything between her and her husband, and she had denied this, although of course this was untrue. Mrs Waite, she added, had three times threatened to commit suicide, the last time being four days before she died. On that occasion Mrs Waite had said that she was losing the use of her hands and legs again. She was very upset, and made a reference to sleeping tablets, saying that 'they would be the easiest way'.

Questioned by Mr James Ross, QC, defending, Judith

Regan said that Waite was very distressed about his wife's
health and did everything that he could for her. He had
injured his back carrying her up and down the stairs to the
flat.

'You wanted to marry this man, did you not?' asked Mr
Ross. 'Did you think there was no hope?'

Miss Regan nodded, but when Mr Justice Willis told her
that she must answer the question, she replied, 'A little
hope, maybe.'

Although Miss Regan told the court that she was alarmed
by Mrs Waite's suicide threats, other witnesses expressed
opposing views on whether or not suicide had indeed been
seriously contemplated by the deceased. Asked whether
the discovery of her husband's affair with another woman
might have driven Mrs Waite to the point of wishing to
commit suicide, Mrs Rosalie Waite, the mother of the
accused, replied, 'It might have done.' Her daughter-in-
law, she added, '. . . just lived for her husband and children, and she must have been very unhappy to learn that
he was being unfaithful to her. She would have done
almost anything to keep her family together.'

Dr Harold Parker testified that Mrs Waite's behaviour
during the time that he was treating her was quite incon-
sistent with her administering poison to herself. 'She fully
co-operated in the treatment,' he said. 'I am sure that she
wanted to recover.'

Mrs Waite's sister, Mrs Jones, told the jury that she had
never heard or seen anything which might have suggested
that her sister would take her own life. 'She was just not
that kind of person,' she said. 'She would have forgiven
anyone who wronged her.'

Dr Barrowcliff, after giving evidence relating to the
arsenic he had found in the dead woman's body and hair,
said that he did not think the poisoning accidental. 'As far
as suicide was concerned,' he continued, 'I think it incon-
ceivable that a person in his or her right mind – and there is
no evidence that the deceased was otherwise – would use
such an unpleasant and painful method. In twenty-five
years' experience I have never yet met with a suicide case
where arsenic was used.'

Waite was now questioned by both counsel about his attitude towards the two women in his life, in particular his feelings towards them in the summer of 1969.

'What were your feelings towards Judith Regan?' asked Mr Ross.

'I was becoming more and more deeply involved,' Waite replied.

'What were your feelings towards your wife?' Mr Ross continued, to which Waite replied,

'They must have been cooling.'

'What positive steps could you have taken about this affair?' persisted Mr Ross.

'First of all,' Waite said, 'I would have to wait until my wife was better; I couldn't leave her as she was.'

'To raise the matter at any time would have caused her considerable distress?' counsel queried.

'Yes. I still wasn't sure I could go through with it. But I was going to try anyway. I knew it couldn't come about until Judith was twenty-one.'

Questioned next about his marital relations, Waite said that he found it impossible to have sexual intercourse with his wife and while at the same time he was becoming more and more deeply involved with Miss Regan. 'I still felt a lot for my wife,' he said. 'I did not want our marriage to end just then. I wanted to make the best of what we had.' He had denied to his wife that there was anything between himself and Judith Regan, and at that time he thought that she believed him, but later he was not so sure. She had spoken of taking some tablets, and several times she had said that she did not wish to be a burden on him and the children. He had told her 'not to be so silly'.

Mr Davies accused Waite of sending hypocritical love letters to his wife while carrying on his affair with Miss Regan. 'Any woman reading those letters,' he said, 'would think she was the only woman in the world, as far as the writer was concerned . . .'

'Yes, she would,' was the reply.

'But she was not the only woman in the world to you, was she?' Mr Davies persisted.

'No,' Waite answered simply.

'You were deceiving your wife by writing her those letters, were you not?' Mr Davies said.

'Isn't it possible to love two people?' Waite replied.

Asked which woman he had put first at that particular time, he replied, 'I cannot say. I just do not know.'

The accused was next asked a number of questions about the poison found at his home. He was asked whether he had warned his family that he was storing such a deadly substance in the flat. His answer to this was that he had not read the warning on the tin which stated that it should not be kept in any building housing human beings or animals.

'I suggest', said Mr Davies, 'that you took it home knowing it to be a deadly poison.'

'I took it home to destroy a wasps' nest,' the accused replied.

Mr Ross, defending, maintained that the case had many inexplicable features. A tin contaminated with Paris Green pesticide had been thrown into a box in an open cupboard at Waite's home, where it had remained until police found it after his wife's death. A guilty man would have been much more likely to have disposed of it as quickly as possible.

Mr Justice Willis, in his summing-up, said that the prosecution's case depended largely on circumstantial evidence. 'There is no derogation of evidence to say that it *is* circumstantial,' he added, 'but it would be wrong to say that it is *merely* circumstantial evidence. It is evidence which has its own peculiar persuasiveness, if you accept it, but different in quality from direct evidence.' He warned the jury: 'You will not condemn this man because he made a young girl half his age his mistress and maintained with her a prolonged clandestine relationship. Nevertheless, it is essential to consider this relationship and such motivating effect as it might have had on the defendant's conduct . . .' He implied that the jury might think it beyond question that Waite, wishing to marry Miss Regan, found that his wife, who refused to divorce him, presented an obstacle in his way.

On 5 March 1970, after a trial which had lasted fifteen

days, the all-male jury found William Waite guilty of killing his wife. He was sentenced to life imprisonment.

I have failed to uncover any record of what happened to Judith Regan. Did she resign herself to waiting out the interminable years of her lover's imprisonment until he should be released, then to rejoin him, or did she bow to the inevitable and find happiness elsewhere? As a practising Catholic, did she feel remorse at having contributed towards his adultery, and bury her grief in a convent? Or did she renounce all intention of marrying another man who was free to make her his wife, counting all lost for love? It is intriguing to speculate on this point. The true romantic would no doubt opt for the first solution to the mystery, but few would not sympathize with the girl who had been swept off her feet by passion.

2

A Constable Named Sherlock

The Red Mini Murder (1967)

The night of 2 March 1967 was pitch-dark and overcast, with no hint of the spring to come, and the narrow lane through Rumerhedge Wood, in Oxfordshire, was, of course, unlit. At ten o'clock that night the trees of the wood loomed through the headlights of the car which Robin Franklin, a fireman, was driving, giving it a most eerie look. Franklin, who lived in Knight's Way, Emmer Green, Berkshire, was driving home with a friend, Colin Pinfield, after a night out at a pub. It was not the most direct route home, but he had decided to take a different road from the way he had come.

The road wound and looped after leaving Hook End as he drove towards Peppard, near Henley-on-Thames, skirted by the lonely wood, when suddenly his headlights picked out the outline of a parked car on a bend, with its sidelights on and its boot open.

'What a stupid place to park a car!' Franklin said, slowing to avoid it. 'The driver obviously doesn't know much about the Highway Code!'

As Franklin came alongside he saw that the car was a blue Cortina, and hardly had he, with some difficulty, managed to edge past the parked vehicle and negotiated the bend when he and his companion noticed a red Mini off the road, which appeared to have run into a tree. A woman was lying beside this car, and the shadowy figure of a man was crouched over her. They also noticed that another man was sitting in the passenger seat of the Mini.

Franklin stopped and the two friends left the car and went over to the scene of the accident to see if they could offer any assistance. The man who had been bending over the woman on the ground straightened himself up. 'No, thank you,' he replied. 'I can manage OK. I'm just going to fetch some towels from my own car.' With these words, the man walked off in the direction of the parked Cortina; but instead of the man coming back with the towels as Franklin expected, he heard the sound of the boot being closed, the door being slammed and a screech of tyres as the car drove off at speed.

Franklin and Pinfield could see that the woman was obviously badly injured, although she seemed to be still alive. They thought it most odd that the driver of the Cortina should have been in such a hurry to drive off. 'Must be one of those blokes who don't want to get involved,' Franklin said.

'Maybe,' his companion said, 'but fancy going off and leaving this poor woman like that – just lying here on the ground. Callous, that's what I call him.'

'There's not a lot we can do,' Franklin said, 'so I think the best thing is to go and call an ambulance. There's a telephone at the AA post a mile or two further on for emergency use.'

Meanwhile, the man who was still sitting in the passenger seat of the Mini did not move or speak, although he did not appear to have been seriously injured; it would seem that he was in a severe state of shock. It transpired later that he had sustained only a minor injury to his left leg.

An ambulance and police soon arrived, and it was established that the man sitting in the Mini was Raymond Sidney Cook, a 32-year-old draughtsman, and that the woman was his wife June Serena, a 41-year-old schoolteacher. The couple lived at Farley View, in Spencer's Wood, a suburb of Reading. That evening they had dined out at the riverside George Hotel in Pangbourne, after which, according to Cook, his wife had started to drive them home. Asked to describe the circumstances of the accident, Cook told doctors at the hospital, where he was treated for the leg injury and shock, that all he could remember was seeing some headlights coming towards him and a tree looming up out of the darkness. He thought that his wife, who had been driving, must have been dazzled by the glare and had driven off the road, running head-on into the tree.

A young constable, appropriately named Stephen Sherlock, was sent from his station at Nettlebed, near Henley-on-Thames, to the scene of the crash to examine the car. Only twenty-six, he had not been a policeman for very long, but he had the same flair for the detection of small and seemingly insignificant clues as his illustrious fictional namesake. He was puzzled to find that, although the Mini had apparently hit the tree head-on, the windshield was intact, and the front part of the car had suffered only minimal damage; in other words, it was what he did *not* find that was significant, much as Conan Doyle's character had pointed out that it was the fact that the dog did *not* bark in the night-time that was important . . .

He then went to the hospital, where he saw the body of Mrs Cook, who had been dead on arrival. The doctors informed him that her injuries could have been caused by her being flung through a windshield and hitting her head on a tree. PC Sherlock said nothing at the time, but nodded non-committally; privately he considered this to have been a physical impossibility.

The following morning, in the early hours, he returned to the scene of the crash; something was nagging persistently at the back of his mind. This was no tragic road accident; there was much more to the crash than met the eye, he thought to himself. He dropped to his hands and knees and examined the road surface minutely with the aid of his flashlight. He found blood on the road more than fifty yards from the Mini. Another officer who had examined the Mini had found that the car was still roadworthy and that it could not have been travelling at more than ten miles an hour when it collided with the tree. Yes, there was something decidedly dodgy about the whole thing, Sherlock mused. And the way the driver of the Cortina had taken off in the manner he did was fishy, too. A bystander who did not wish to become involved would not have stopped at all, never mind parked his car on a bend with the boot up and only sidelights on . . .

Dr Derek Barrowcliff, the Home Office pathologist who,

as we have seen, also officiated in the previous case, after
his post-mortem on Mrs Cook's body was able to inform
detectives that she had died from a compound fracture of
the skull and that there had been seven separate head
injuries. There were no traces of glass, gravel, soil or tree
bark in the wounds, and Dr Barrowcliff did not believe that
she had been in the car when any of her injuries had been
caused. The wounds that caused her death, he averred,
were consistent with her having been hit on the head by a
blunt instrument.

Detective Chief Inspector Wooldridge, of Reading CID,
was quickly convinced that the alleged accident was beginning to look much more like an elaborate cover-up for
murder, and he decided to call in Scotland Yard. Within a
day or two Detective Superintendent (later Deputy Assistant Commissioner) Ian Forbes, accompanied by Detective
Sergeant Peter Hill, arrived in Reading to take charge of
inquiries. On their instructions the funeral, which had been
arranged to take place in Mrs Cook's parish church on 10
March, was stopped and an appeal made for the driver of
the blue Cortina seen parked at the scene of the crash to
come forward.

Raymond Cook stuck doggedly to his story of an accident, but the police did not for one moment believe him,
and he was arrested outside Reading Coroner's Court a few
moments after the inquest had been opened and adjourned
until 17 March. Told that he would be charged with the
murder of his wife, Cook replied, 'You must be joking.'

The circumstances in which the driver of the Cortina had
left the scene were so suspicious that nationwide inquiries
were launched to trace the car, and eventually, after a good
deal of painstaking legwork on the part of the police and
some leads from witnesses who had been in the area on the
night in question, the blue Cortina was traced. The car,
licence number 7711 FM, was registered to a 46-year-old
plant manager named Eric Jones, of Chester Road, Wrexham, Denbighshire, more than a hundred miles away from
lonely Rumerhedge Wood. A local police officer, Detective
Sergeant Charles Matthews, who knew Jones personally,
was asked to interview him. Jones was emphatic that he

had not been anywhere near Reading on 2 March. 'You'll find nothing here,' he said – a statement which Matthews found odd, and which made him suspicious; Matthews had not told Jones he was looking for anything, although he had been asked by the Reading police to search Jones's premises. He was also asked to examine his car. Again, as in the case of PC Sherlock earlier in the investigation, it was what Matthews could *not* find that reinforced his suspicions: he could not locate the jack, which was missing from the Cortina. Matthews knew that Jones travelled considerable distances in the course of his work, and what car driver goes any distance without a jack?

A car jack could, the pathologist said after the autopsy, have been employed to bludgeon Mrs Cook to death; her injuries were consistent with the use of such an instrument. If indeed this has been the case, it was more than likely that Jones would have disposed of it in the vicinity of his home. Frogmen were called in to search ponds and lakes in the immediate area, and their efforts soon yielded results: the missing jack was discovered at the bottom of a lake called Gresford Flash just outside Wrexham.

In the mean time, a witness had been found who had seen the blue Cortina in the Reading area on the night in question. He did not know the man who was driving the car, but he did know the passenger – a blonde named Valerie Newell, who was known as Kim. The girl, who was twenty-three, lived next door to his mother in Sidmouth Street, Reading.

The pieces of the jigsaw were beginning to come together, although a few were still missing. By the time this further sighting came to light, the police had already discovered that Raymond Cook and Valerie, or Kim, Newell had met at a hospital where both had worked as nurses. For several months prior to the alleged accident they had been lovers. They had made no secret of their affair, nor of the fact that Cook's wife June was in the way, and they had told several of their friends that they would like to marry, if Cook were free. It was also quickly discovered that Eric Jones had been a former lover of Kim Newell.

Just before Christmas 1966 Cook and Newell visited a

Jamaican friend, Cleland Thompson, who lived in the Southcote area of Reading. At that meeting, Kim told him that she herself would willingly kill Mrs Cook if she thought that she could get away with it, adding almost as an afterthought, 'If you know anyone who would do the job it would pay them to do it.' The mind boggles when considering how remarkably indiscreet this girl was in her statements, made in all seriousness, to her friends.

During the same period a conversation took place between Eric Jones and Kim Newell in the presence of a Mrs Susan Heslop, who at that time was staying with Kim. One evening Jones, Kim Newell and her friend Susan Heslop drove to an old disused airfield which had been described by Kim as a 'suitable quiet place'. There was talk between Jones and Kim of giving Mrs Cook drink while she was out in her own car so that she would lose control and run it into the river. In fact Mrs Heslop gained the distinct impression that her two companions were plotting to engineer the 'accidental' drowning of Mrs Cook.

After Raymond Cook's arrest, Kim visited her sister, Mrs Janet Adams, of Lower Way, Thatcham, Berkshire. Perhaps because she was very scared by that time, and felt that she must unburden herself of her guilt to someone close to her, she confessed that the 'accident' was in fact a prearranged murder plot hatched by Cook, Jones and herself, and that the killing of Mrs Cook had actually been carried out by Jones. Following this visit, however, Kim had second thoughts about her confession, even to the extent of denying that she was having an affair with Raymond Cook. Brazening it out, she said, 'I admit that we were friends, but I was no more friendly with him than I was with his wife.' All this, however, was not going to help her in the end.

Mrs Adams spent several days in a state of agonized indecision; Kim was, after all, her own sister. But eventually conscience won the day, and she walked into Reading police station to tell them the whole story. On 18 April 1967, just one month after Raymond Cook had been arrested, Eric Jones and Kim Newell were also charged with the murder of June Cook.

Kim and her sister Janet had grown up on a farm at Rhos-y-Madoc, near Ruabon in Denbighshire. When Kim was fifteen, she had met Eric Jones, a tree-feller, who supplemented his income by performing illegal abortions. The following year Kim was already pregnant by him, but his abilities as an abortionist put paid to her dilemma by disposing of the unwanted result of their association. Three years later, she left home to become a children's nurse in Oxford. She soon lost not only her Welsh accent but any inhibitions remaining from her strict Welsh upbringing. She associated with wealthy young men who were undergraduates at the university, a racehorse breeder, a bookmaker and other well-heeled boyfriends. Four more times she became pregnant, and four more times Eric Jones was called in to perform abortions. One would have thought that, along with her new-found sophistication and free-and-easy lifestyle, she would have learned something about birth control.

From Oxford she moved to Reading, where she continued her life of shallow gaiety, developing a taste for luxury and preying on rich businessmen who were able to indulge her. At one stage she became engaged to the son of a police officer, but this was broken off when her fiancé discovered that there had never been a time when she had had fewer than a minimum of two lovers at a time, and that their engagement had not altered the status quo one whit.

In 1966 Kim gave up being a children's nurse to take up a nursing position at Borocourt Hospital, a mental institution near Reading. It was here that she met Raymond Cook, a male nurse, who at six feet 4 inches tall and balding, would not, on the face of it, have seemed a likely candidate for the petite Kim Newell's attentions, but since he was a free spender she might at first have believed him to be wealthy. His wife June, who was nine years older, was a teacher of mentally handicapped children, and it was she who had persuaded him to embark upon his new career of mental nursing. He had previously worked at the Handley–Page aircraft factory at Woodley, near Reading, as a draughtsman.

Cook enrolled as a student nurse, and his reduced financial status did not make such a tremendous difference, because their house had been an outright gift from his wife's parents, so they had no mortgage worries. June, moreover, had other assets in the form of property, insurance, stocks and shares, and cash in the bank, worth altogether some £11,000.

Within a few weeks of their first meeting, Cook and Kim became lovers. Cook was quite besotted with the blonde gold-digging beauty, and before long he had cashed in a £700 insurance policy in order to give her the things she craved: good clothes, expensive French perfumes, meals and drinks at the best hotels, and so on. It was nothing unusual for him to spend thirty pounds a week on her, and within four months the £700 had vanished into thin air.

After studying three years for his nursing examinations, Cook failed them miserably, doubtless distracted by the seductive Kim. He failed also in an application to re-enrol for a further course, and resigned his post in disgust. Kim became pregnant at the same time, and lost her own job. Mrs Cook found out about their association, and made a new will, under the terms of which all her property was to be held in trust for their two children, cutting her husband out altogether.

Cook left his wife and moved in with Kim. By now cash was running short. Kim made another trip to see Eric Jones, but this time Cook went with her. The three of them met in a Chinese restaurant just before Christmas 1966. Asked whether she had come to ask him for yet another abortion, Kim told Jones, 'No, not this time. We want you to do a much more difficult job – we want you to bump off Ray's old woman.' Jones was given one hundred pounds in cash as a deposit, and promised one thousand pounds when the job was done. Several alternative plots were discussed, and it was eventually decided that a fake car accident would be the best method, because Mrs Cook held an insurance policy which would pay out one thousand pounds in the event of her death by accident.

First of all, however, they had to ensure that the money would be paid to Cook after his wife's death. So the scheming pair concocted an elaborate ploy: Cook would return to his wife and tell her that he had ended his association with Kim Newell. This he did, and June Cook was gullible enough to believe him. She made a new will, which effectively rescinded the previous one and under which her husband would once more be the main beneficiary.

The evening of 2 March 1967 was chosen for the occasion of a celebration of what Mrs Cook thought was her husband's return to the family to make a new start. She arranged for a babysitter to look after the children during their proposed outing, and she had a special hair-do before leaving.

Three versions of the plot to get rid of Mrs Cook, and three versions of the events on the night of her death, were heard when Cook, Jones and Newell stood in the dock before Mr Justice Stable and a jury of ten men and two women at Oxfordshire Assizes in June 1967. Jones and Cook were jointly charged with Mrs Cook's murder; Newell, originally also accused of murder, was charged with being an accessory before the fact, in that she 'counselled, procured and hired' the two men to commit the murder. At first all three pleaded not guilty, but Eric Jones later changed his plea to guilty and was sentenced to life imprisonment. He was then called as a witness for the prosecution.

Jones told the court that when he met Newell and Cook in December 1966 he asked her if she required another abortion, and she replied, 'No – something bigger'. She then said that she wanted him to smash up a Mini car, because she and her lover intended to get rid of Mrs Cook so that they could marry. Several plans were made. On one occasion, Newell showed Jones a narrow humpback bridge and asked him whether, at that spot, he could run Mrs Cook off the road into the river. He told her that the water was not deep enough.

Describing the events of 2 March, Jones said that he picked up Miss Newell in Reading, and she showed him the direction in which the Mini would be coming. She then pointed out the tree into which he was to run the car.

I asked her how on earth she expected a Mini to run into a tree
and kill Mrs Cook [he continued]. She was evasive, and said
that all I had to worry about was to run the Mini into the tree
and help Cook make it look like an accident. Then I was to hit
him as though he had been knocked out. I kept finding
excuses, and she got mad. I said I would get into trouble with
my wife if I did not get back by midnight, and she replied that I
would get in a bloody sight more trouble if I left. She reminded
me that I could get eight years for abortion, and said that she
had policemen in Reading who used to go up to her flat for
coffee at night, and they would expose me.

After examining the tree, Jones said that he drove Newell
back to Reading and then returned to the appointed place.
When the red Mini came along, Cook stopped, left the car
and went over to where Jones was standing beside his
parked Cortina pretending that his car had broken down,
and told him to 'get on with it'. They both went over to the
Mini, and Cook called to his wife and asked her whether
she would mind giving Jones a lift into town as his car had
packed up on him.

Mr Brian Gibbens, QC, leading for the Crown, asked
Jones: 'Is it right that you struck Mrs Cook with an
implement?'

The witness replied, 'Yes, I did.'

'Did Mr Cook take any part in the actual violence against
Mrs Cook?'

'None, sir,' Jones replied. 'He handed me the car jack,
with which I struck Mrs Cook.'

He went on to describe how he had run the Mini into the
tree with Cook and his wife both in the vehicle. He stood on
the running-board on the driver's side, and, having opened
the door, put one foot on the accelerator and one hand
on the steering-wheel while Cook started the ignition and
put the car in gear. Later, when Mrs Cook was lying on
the ground, he hit her again with the jack.

Cross-examined by Mr Douglas Draycott, QC, for Cook,
Jones agreed that nothing was said in Cook's presence
about killing Mrs Cook when there was talk of 'getting rid of
her'. Miss Newell had told him that 'Cook would not have
the guts'.

'Are you telling the jury that Miss Newell forced you?' Mr Draycott asked.

'In a way, yes.'

'The reason that you are saying this is to make your position seem better?' Mr Draycott queried.

'No, sir.'

'You can say that you were not intending to kill, but that by an amazing piece of sheer bad luck at that particular moment a car jack was put into your hand?' counsel persisted.

'Yes,' Jones replied.

During his cross-examination Cook stated that he was terrified and that he did not remember starting the car. 'Jones was pressing the accelerator,' he said, 'and the Mini went forward and collided with a tree . . . I hit my head on some part of the car and found myself on the road, and I lost consciousness. When I came to I returned to the car. My wife wasn't in the car, but I could hear the sound of her heavy breathing. Jones had a car jack in his hand. Then he left, and the lights of another car appeared'.

Cook agreed that he did not make any serious attempt to stop Jones. 'I have never used violence against anybody,' he said. 'I have never been in a fight with anybody.'

Mr Gibbens held up the car jack in court. It was a dramatic moment as he held the instrument of death aloft.

'Here is a man', he said, 'slaughtering your wife, and because you had never used violence to anybody before you didn't think of trying to save your wife?'

Cook did not reply.

Mr Gibbens pressed his point more strongly. 'Do I take it that you made no effort to defend your wife?'

'I made some kind of effort,' replied Cook lamely.

'You made no attempt whatsoever!' retorted Mr Gibbens.

'I made a very little attempt,' insisted Cook.

Replying to Mr Howard, Cook said that he was very frightened of Jones, having seen what he had done that night.

On the ninth day of the trial Kim Newell, wearing a maternity smock, went into the witness-box, and was given a pile of cushions to sit on while she gave evidence for the next two days, answering a barrage of questions from three counsels and the judge. She stated that she had met Jones and drove with him to Rumerhedge Wood a few hours before the crime. She asked him what he was going to do, and he told her that the less she knew about it the better, and he then drove her back to Reading.

'Mr Cook rang me at 4.30 p.m. the next day,' she went on. 'I knew that he had been involved in an accident, because somebody told me. I bought the local paper. When Mr Cook rang me I asked him whether he had been injured, and he said that he was OK except for a bump on the head and a leg injury which was not too bad. I asked him about Mrs Cook, and he said, "Oh, I'd rather not talk about that." He sounded very distressed . . . The next day was Saturday. He came to see me, and he was very upset and did not want to talk about what had happened.'

Continuing her evidence, she said that after Cook had been arrested she saw Jones and asked him how he had killed Mrs Cook. He told her that he had hit Mrs Cook with a car jack, and warned her that she '. . . had better not tell the police or else'. She said that she was very frightened.

Mr Draycott then asked the witness whether she thought that, from her knowledge of Cook, he would have driven with his wife through the wood if he had known that she was going to be harmed. Miss Newell said no. 'Are you suggesting, then,' Mr Draycott continued, 'that Cook was the prime mover in the arrangements with Jones and that you were merely on the sidelines?' The witness replied in the affirmative.

'A reversal, I suggest, of the true situation?'

'No.'

When Newell again denied that she knew what Jones was intending to do to Mrs Cook, Mr Justice Stable asked her, 'You are saying that all these negotiations were going on behind your back?'

'They must have been,' she replied.

Summing up for the Crown, Mr Gibbens said that Newell was the one who provided the motive and the means, while she herself kept safe and sound behind the scenes. He pointed out that Cook was utterly besotted with her, and in her grip. While he had nothing else in mind but love and marriage, Newell was far more interested in money and an easy life.

On the thirteenth day of the trial, during the judge's summing-up, Newell sat weeping in the dock. However, she showed no sign of emotion when the jury, after a three-hour retirement, found both her and Cook guilty as charged. Commenting that it was in his discretion to pass the same sentence in each case, Mr Justice Stable said that he was sentencing them both to life imprisonment. He commended the police team which had investigated the murder, making particular reference to Sherlock, but for whose perspicacity this so-called 'accident' might have escaped further investigation.

On 9 August 1967, seven weeks after she was sentenced, Kim Newell gave birth to a 6-pound son, who was christened Paul, and later adopted. Five months after the birth, the Court of Criminal Appeal dismissed applications for leave to appeal by both Newell and Cook, the father of her child.

3

Passion vs. Promotion

James Ronald Robertson (1950)

The county of Oxford does not have the monopoly of alert bobbies. Another astute policeman, William Kevan, whose beat took him through some of the worst parts of Glasgow's slum district of the Gorbals, refused to accept at its face value the too obvious evidence before him when he came upon the bloody and mangled body of a woman lying on the road on the outskirts of the city. He had been called to the scene by a cab-driver who had found her while driving along Prospect Hill Road on his way to Glasgow from Kilmarnock. John Kennedy, the cabbie, had noted the time of his discovery as 12.55 a.m., which PC Kevan duly noted in his log-book under the date, 28 July 1950. The cabbie told him that he thought the woman must have been struck by a heavy lorry travelling at speed.

It was obvious to PC Kevan that the victim was dead, and equally obvious that she had been killed by a vehicle; tyre marks were clearly visible on the body. But there was something very odd about them: they were quite distinct, but they were not parallel, and at one point they actually crossed each other. Dropping to his hands and knees to examine the scene more closely with his flashlight, PC Kevan found more tyre marks further along the road, indicating that a car had made a U-turn on the grass verge running alongside.

Constable Kevan was very puzzled, more by what he failed to find rather than by what he found, just as in the case of Constable Sherlock in the Red Mini case described in the last chapter. The more Constable Kevan was puzzled the more suspicious he became. As an experienced traffic policeman he knew that when a vehicle hits a pedestrian with the degree of violence evident in this case, the impact almost invariably does some damage to the vehicle, shattering glass or at least chipping paint from the bodywork. He switched on the brilliant headlamps of his patrol car and went over every inch of the road illuminated by their beams. He found nothing – not even any pieces of dried mud which are normally dislodged from the underside of any vehicle involved in such a collision.

Constable Kevan contacted the CID, and Detective Chief Inspector Donald McDougal decided, on this evidence, to treat the supposed accident as a case of murder . . .

The suspicions of the police were quickly justified by the findings of forensic experts Professor Andrew Allison and Dr James Imrie, who performed the post-mortem on the victim's body. They announced that they had never seen a road accident victim with the type of injuries sustained by the woman in this case. There was a total of thirty separate external wounds, as well as severe internal injuries, but only superficial grazing on the legs. When a person is knocked down by a vehicle, the legs are usually struck by some part of the car, but there was no evidence on this woman's legs to indicate an impact that could have thrown her to the ground.

There were some more sinister discoveries: some of the injuries, including a crushed pelvis, had been inflicted after death; and there was a large bruise on the right temple, which did not fit into the pattern of the other injuries she had sustained – in fact, it appeared to have been caused by a blow from a blunt instrument. On the basis of the purely medical evidence, it looked as though after the woman had been knocked out, she had been placed on the road while still unconscious and then run over twice by a car, once while she was still alive, and a second time after death.

An examination of the tyre marks ruled out the possibility that the victim had been run over and killed by a car and subsequently run over by a second vehicle while lying dead on the road. All the tyre tracks matched exactly and had been made by the same car; moreover, the car had been travelling first one way and then, after making a U-turn, from the opposite direction.

There was nothing on the victim to identify her, but police speculation was soon ended when at 8 a.m. a Mrs Rose O'Donnell, of Rutherglen Road, Glasgow, called in at her nearest police station. She said that she was very worried because her friend, Catherine McCluskey, had failed to collect her two children, six-year-old Patrick and baby John, aged three months, whom she had left with Mrs O'Donnell the previous evening while she went out to enjoy an evening at the pub. Mrs O'Donnell told a police officer that she had looked after the children on several previous occasions when her friend, who was an unmarried mother, went out, but never before had Miss McCluskey failed to collect the children afterwards and take them home to her house in Nicholson Street.

It soon became clear from Mrs O'Donnell's description of the missing woman – aged forty, blonde, and wearing a red coat and white shoes – that she was the woman who had been found in Prospect Hill Road a few hours earlier. Later that same day Mrs O'Donnell identified her friend's body at the city mortuary, and afterwards police asked her whether she knew the names of any of the dead woman's men friends or acquaintances. Mrs O'Donnell replied, 'She told me that she was going out with a bobby who's on point duty in the Gorbals. That's the only one I can think of.'

Further information linking the victim with a police officer was given by Mrs Grace Johnstone, a neighbour in Nicholson Street. She informed detectives that Miss McCluskey had told her that the father of the older boy was an American GI and that the baby's father was a policeman, who had agreed to pay her maintenance. Miss Jean Dickson, a clerical officer with the Glasgow Assistance Board, stated that Catherine McCluskey had applied for assistance after the birth of her second child. At the time she had refused to name the father, but eventually she admitted that he was a policeman who was sometimes on duty near her home, although she still would not name him.

It was not difficult to trace the police officer concerned. At a time when a Glasgow constable's pay was only six to seven pounds a week, very few of them were able to run a car, but one constable was known to use a large black

Austin. He was James Ronald Robertson, aged thirty-three, who was married and the father of two children.

PC Robertson had been on duty on the night of 27 to 28 July. During that week he had been patrolling his beat with PC Dugald Moffatt, who recalled that at about 11.15 p.m. on 27 July his partner had left the beat after saying, with a wink, 'I'm just going to nip off and take a blonde home.' Robertson went off in his Austin car, licence number DYS 570, in which he had arrived for duty that night. Moffatt did not see him again until he reported back at 1.10 a.m. Moffatt noticed that his fellow officer was drenched with sweat, dishevelled and dusty. The truant officer explained his unkempt appearance by stating that the exhaust pipe of his car had broken and that he had had to get down on the ground and tie it up with string.

Before examining Robertson's car, which was kept in a garage in Gorbals Street, near his home in Hillingdon Road, detectives made a routine check of the licence number with the vehicle registration records. They were amazed to find that it had been issued to a farmer in Aberdeenshire for a tractor, and that the car itself had been stolen some months previously from a solicitor in Lanarkshire. Robertson, when questioned on these points, admitted quite frankly that he had 'found the car abandoned', had failed to report it, and had then changed its number plates for some he had taken from an unattended tractor he had seen in a field. On his own admission he was a thief, but this did not make him a murderer . . .

The car was then examined by Sergeant McCallum of the Traffic Division. The bodywork was undamaged and showed no sign of having struck anything or anybody, but when the underside was examined the exhaust pipe was found to be broken, and there were traces of blood, skin and hair. McCallum had previously looked very carefully at the road surface where the woman's body was found, and had noticed some odd scrape marks near the tyre impressions. He took the Austin back to the murder scene and was able to prove that these scrapes had been made by the broken exhaust pipe touching the ground as the car went over the body.

Robertson was arrested while on duty on the night after the murder. He admitted at once that Catherine McCluskey had been killed by the car he was driving, but insisted that it had been an accident. He said that he had known her for about a year since going to investigate a disturbance at the house where she was living, but denied that they were on intimate terms, and rejected emphatically the suggestion that he was the father of her baby.

He said that on the night of 27 July he had met her casually and she had told him that she had been turned out of her lodgings. She had asked him to drive her to a village some miles outside the city, but he refused, saying that he could not be absent from his beat for so long. He did, however, agree to take her to some friends who lived much nearer, and who would put her up temporarily. As they drove along Prospect Hill Road they had an argument, and he told her to get out and walk. She left the car in a huff and he started to drive off, then thought better of it and reversed the car with the idea of picking her up again. Suddenly, he said, he felt a bump, and at the same time noticed a sharp increase in the exhaust noise. He stopped the car and alighted to investigate, and found Miss McCluskey lying partly underneath the car. He tried to pull her clear, but he could not do so because her clothing was caught in the propeller shaft. He returned to the car and moved it backwards and forwards several times in an attempt to free her, but when at last he succeeded he discovered that she was dead. Overwhelmed by the realization of the invidiousness of his position, he returned to his car and drove off.

It was, of course, an incredibly stupid explanation, and it was nothing short of amazing that Robertson thought that anyone would believe it. Even the most dim-witted learner-driver would scarcely have tried to free an injured person caught under a car by driving it backwards and forwards over the person's body; how much less likely would it be that a tough Glasgow policeman with considerable experience of road accidents should perform such a senseless action, let alone have any hope that his superiors would believe his story. If the constable's account had been true, he would have had only to report the accident and help would have been immediately forthcoming.

In fact, Robertson did report it – but in a very different way from his statement at the police station. Five days later, on 3 August, another police officer opened the log-book in the Cumberland Street police box, and there found the following entry:

> At 2.30 a.m. to-day, 28 July, a woman was knocked down in Prospect Hill-rd., near Aikenhead-rd., by a motorcar believed to be a small blue Austin, maybe 10 hp, driven by a man wearing a light fawn Burberry-type coat. The car did not stop. Last seen driving towards the city in Aikenhead-rd.

The report was signed by James Ronald Robertson.

When arrested, Robertson was found to be carrying a heavy rubber truncheon, which was not part of the regulation equipment of a Glasgow beat policeman. There was further damning evidence, of a negative kind, in the complete lack of bloodstains on his shoes or uniform; in view of the mangling injuries to the victim, it was obvious that no one could have touched her without some transference of blood. Yet microscopic examination failed to reveal even the tiniest spot of blood on Robertson's clothing.

His story about the woman's clothes' having become entangled in the propeller shaft was quickly scotched by forensic experts, who could not find even the smallest trace of cloth fibres on the propeller shaft, nor any microscopic fragments of metal, rust or other material from the shaft on her clothing. In addition to this, a witness at the subsequent trial, Mr Charles Wicks, a consulting engineer from Edinburgh, pointed out that the propeller shaft in the Austin was enclosed. 'I do not see how it could have been possible', he testified, 'for her clothes to have become entangled in this manner.'

Robertson's trial for the murder of Catherine McCluskey took place in the Glasgow High Court in November 1950 before a jury of eight men and seven women. During the six-day trial two pathologists described their findings, and Mr John (later Lord) Cameron, for the defence, said that a small dent in the rear bumper of the car could have been caused by the impact of a human bone. Professor John Glaister, the famous expert in medical jurisprudence, agreed that such a dent could be caused in that way, but it would cause a definite and extensive bruise, and such a bruise was not found among the woman's many injuries. He told the court: 'I can account for most of these by a forward running-down on more than one occasion . . . I am forced to the conclusion that the body must have been in a recumbent position when the car struck it the first time.'

A possible motive for murder was suggested by the Crown counsel, Mr H. Leslie, KC, who submitted that there was an intimate bond between Robertson and Miss McCluskey, which he was trying to sever and she was attempting to maintain. Robertson was known to be ambitious, and the theory was that he felt that his liaison with the dead woman would prove an obstacle to the pursuit of his career. A married man with two children, he had been at pains to keep secret his association with the unmarried mother of two.

It is probable that an argument had flared up while Robertson and the deceased woman were driving along in his car. This argument, it seemed, would most likely have arisen over the question of maintenance for the baby, which Robertson, it was alleged, had agreed to pay; if this were true, this could imply that Robertson had admitted to being the father of Miss McCluskey's second child. She, unlike Robertson, did not have a career at stake, and had told several people that the child was his. In Robertson's case, however, such an admission would have been one more nail in the coffin of his promotion prospects. Throughout his entire trial Robertson insisted that his relationship with Miss McCluskey had been no more than a casual one, and a platonic one at that. No one in the courtroom believed him.

The jury decided by a majority verdict that Robertson was guilty of murder, and he was hanged in Barlinnie Prison in Glasgow on 15 December 1950. One thing only is certain amid all the uncertainties in this case: had he not made the mistake of running the car over his victim twice – presumably to make sure that she was dead and could not give evidence against him – it is unlikely that he would have been suspected of any involvement. The double set of tyre marks, spotted by an alert copper, was the first clue which led inevitably to the chain of forensic evidence which eventually sent Robertson to the gallows.

4

Take a Letter, Miss Smith

Madeleine Smith (1857)

Still in Glasgow, but now just over one hundred years
earlier, in 1855, we find that passion could rear its insistent
head with as much intensity in the breast of a lady of the
more genteel upper classes as it could in her more plebeian
sisters. The only difference was that a lady from a more
educated background could put it into words, and in fact
the more articulate the passion-smitten lady the more
devastating the results were likely to be.

One such lady was Madeleine Smith, the daughter of a
wealthy architect, who was eighteen at the time this story
opens. The Smiths lived at 7 Blythswood Square in Glasgow, and they also had a country house on the Clyde,
named Rowaleyn, which the architect had designed himself. The family seemed to spend a good deal of its time
flitting from one home to the other.

In those days it was the custom for society ladies to walk,
suitably chaperoned, in Glasgow's fashionable Sauchiehall
Street on fine days. Thus it was that Madeleine,
chaperoned by her sister Bessie, would take the air, not
unmindful of admiring glances from passing gentlemen, of
course. Since Madeleine and her sister frequently attended
various society functions, dances and parties given by
friends of her father, it was quite commonplace for some of
the gentlemen who had been their dancing partners at such
gatherings to be taking the air at the same time and thus in a
position to meet and speak to the two sisters when they
recognized each other in the street.

It so happened that on one of these occasions a young
man named Robert Baird, who knew Bessie Smith from
having met her at one of these parties, was walking in

Sauchiehall Street, accompanied by a friend, Pierre Emile L'Angelier, when they met Bessie and Madeleine. Robert Baird introduced his companion to the two girls, little knowing what train of events he had set in motion.

L'Angelier, who was known as Emile rather than Pierre, was a native of Jersey, although his father had been born in France but had left that country during the revolution of 1830 and settled in Jersey. Emile was a great romantic and not only claimed that he was a Frenchman from France but claimed kinship with various members of the old French aristocracy – claims which few could go to the trouble of disproving, especially the gullible females who were flattered by his attentions. What very few of these ladies knew was that Emile was a humble clerk in a seed merchants' office in Bothwell Street, earning the princely sum of ten shillings a week. But no one would have guessed this, judging from his high-flown manner of talking and the fancy, almost dandyish style of dress which he affected.

Madeleine Smith gave the impression of an almost aristocratic air of good breeding which radiated from her deportment long before Emile had heard her speech, and it was this that attracted him irresistibly to her rather than her admittedly not inconsiderable beauty.

Madeleine, for her part, was also irresistibly drawn to the handsome stranger. He had all the attractions of an older man (he was ten years Madeleine's senior), with his polished manners and air of *savoire-faire*. He professed to be a Frenchman – a potent lure for the romantically inclined young ladies of leisure who had little more to do than read Victorian novels which hinted darkly, if euphemistically, that the French were wonderful lovers, as opposed to their more prosaic counterparts across the Channel. He was also handsome.

Emile and Madeleine contrived a number of further meetings, always, in her case, respectably chaperoned by Bessie, although Emile was not always in the company of his friend Robert Baird. As their friendship progressed, Bessie was doubtless enjoined to secrecy about these meetings, and probably, as young girls will, entered into the conspiracy of silence with a certain amount of enjoyment, tempered possibly by her own feelings of admiration for the object of her sister's attentions. But Bessie knew she had no chance: plain and dumpy, she could not hold a candle to Madeleine's slender attractions.

It was not long before the regular strolls in Sauchiehall Street had to be given up in favour of an enforced stay in the family's country house, Rowaleyn. Madeleine now had no alternative but to keep in touch with her new friend by post, but she would have to be very circumspect, since her father would certainly not approve of his daughter's growing friendship with an almost penniless clerk, however well intentioned. Madeleine herself, when she learned of her friend's humble status in life, found this romantic, redolent of those novels she had read in which poverty-stricken geniuses languished in bare attics. No, it would never do for her father to discover that she was receiving regular letters in the flowing handwriting of a Gallic admirer.

Madeleine's first letter ran, in part, as follows (I have made one or two very slight amendments in order to clarify ambiguities in the original):

Rowaleyn [undated]

My dear Emile,

I do not feel as if I were writing you for the first time. Though our acquaintance has been very short, yet we have become as familiar friends. May we long continue so. And ere long may you be a friend of Papa's is my most earnest desire. We feel it rather dull here after the excitement of town life. But then we have much more time to devote to study and improvement. I often wish you were near us, we could take such charming walks. One enjoys walking with a pleasant companion, and where could we find one equal to yourself?

We shall be in town next-week. We are going to the Ball on the 20th of this month, so we will be several times in Glasgow before that. Papa and Mama are going to town next Sunday. So of course you do *not* come to Rowaleyn. We shall not expect you. Bessie desires me to remember her to you. Write on Wednesday or Thursday. I must now say adieu.

With kind love, believe me,

Yours very sincerely,
Madeleine.

This semi-formal style was of fleeting duration. We are told that L'Angelier answered Madeleine's letter, but his reply is not in existence – perhaps she destroyed it lest it should fall into wrong hands. All her prudence, however, was wasted, for it seemed that Bessie, in a fit of petulance (could it have been jealousy?) 'blabbed' to her father about her sister's new-found association. This can be seen from the next letter, also undated, that Madeleine wrote to L'Angelier. It was, like her first missive, addressed to him care of his office address at 10 Bothwell Street, Glasgow. Both these letters were sent in the early part of April 1855.

The letter reads:

Rowaleyn [undated]

My dear Emile,

Many thanks for your kind epistle. We are to be in town to-morrow (Wednesday). Bessie said I was not to let you know. But I must tell you why! She was *kind* enough to tell Papa that you were in the habit of walking with us. Papa was very angry with me for walking with a gentleman unknown to him. I told him he had been introduced, and I saw no harm in it. Bessie joins with Papa and blames me for the whole affair. She does not know I am writing you, so don't mention it.

We are to call at 7 Blythswood Square on Wednesday about a quarter past 12 o'clock. So if you could be in Mr McCall's lodgings – see us come out of Mrs Ramsay's – come after us – say you are astonished to see us in town without letting you know – and we shall see how Bessie acts . . . We are to be in town all night.

Rest assured I shall not mention to anyone that you have written me. I know from experience that the world is not lenient in its observations. But I don't care for the world's remarks so long as my own heart tells me I am doing nothing wrong. Only if the day is fine expect us to-morrow. Not a word of this letter. Adieu till we meet.

Believe me,
Yours most sincerely,
Madeleine.

It had not taken Mr Smith long to discover that this forward young man was a ten-shillings-a-week clerk in Huggins the seed merchants'. Like any other Victorian paterfamilias, his word was law, and as a wealthy architect with prominent social standing he would, typically, deem that this impoverished young upstart – and a foreigner to boot – was completely unfit as a suitor for Madeleine's hand. Her mother was more sad than angry; she was a chronic invalid who left the running of the household to Madeleine, and doubtless realized that such a marriage would deprive her of her economic advantage of having one of her daughters as housekeeper. Torn between loyalty to her parents, fear of her father and pity for her mother on the one hand, and her growing affection for L'Angelier on the other, Madeleine was forced to make an agonizing decision. She decided that it would be prudent to write to L'Angelier and tell him that it would be better if their correspondence were to end. This letter she wrote to him at his lodgings in the Botanic Gardens, on the Great Western Road.

Rowaleyn, 18 April 1855

My dear Emile,
   I now perform the promise I made in parting to write you soon. We are to be in Glasgow to-morrow (Thursday). But as my time shall not be at my own disposal, I cannot fix any time to see you. Chance may throw you in my way.
   I think you will agree with me in what I intend proposing, viz., that for the present the correspondence had better *stop*. I know your good feeling will not take this unkindly, it is meant quite the reverse. By continuing to correspond harm may arise. In *dis*continuing it nothing can be said . . .

It would appear that L'Angelier lost or destroyed the remaining portion of this letter, for it has never come to light.
   However, even if the correspondence stopped, the pair still met after the family had returned to Glasgow. L'Angelier took to hanging around Blythswood Square at all kinds of hours, in the hope of seeing Madeleine by chance. In this he succeeded, and thus began the clandestine meetings which enabled the ill-starred sweethearts to snatch a few moments of happiness. Madeleine took quite a few risks, letting him into the house by the rear entrance when the coast was clear, but she was always fearful of discovery: there were the servants as well as the family to

watch out for. The kitchen or the laundry were the spots least likely to be disturbed late at night, but they were not completely safe. It must have been a nerve-racking experience kissing her swain and listening out for ominous footfalls at the same time.

Meanwhile L'Angelier had struck up a friendship with an elderly maiden lady, a Miss Mary Perry, at the Episcopal church which he attended, St Jude's. Miss Perry often invited L'Angelier to tea at her house at 144 Renfrew Street. He confided in her that he was deeply in love with Miss Madeleine Smith, the daughter of a wealthy architect, and that her father was putting difficulties in their way. Miss Perry, who despite her seventy years was a romantic soul, suggested that he invited Miss Smith to take tea with him at her house on his next visit. He warmly agreed.

Miss Perry took an instant liking to Madeleine who, in her turn, found her new acquaintance quickly becoming a bosom friend, and as often as she could manage it she would keep her assignations with L'Angelier at 144 Renfrew Street, while Miss Perry kept discreetly out of the way. By this time L'Angelier was calling Madeleine by the French pet name of 'Mimi'.

In July 1855 Madeleine's father discovered that, although the correspondence had stopped, she was still seeing L'Angelier in secret; how he found out is not known. There was a scene, during which Mr Smith forbade his daughter to see the young man again or to communicate with him in any way. All she could do was write a despairing letter to Miss Perry.

7 Blythswood Square
[undated]

Dearest Miss Perry,
    Many kind thanks for all your kindness to me. Emile will tell you I have bid him adieu. My Papa would not give his consent, so I am in duty bound to obey him. Comfort dear Emile. It is a heavy blow to us both. I had hoped some day to have been happy with him, but, alas! it was not intended. We were doomed to be disappointed. You have been a kind friend to him. Oh! continue so. I hope and trust he may prosper . . . Think my conduct not unkind. I have a father to please, and a

kind father too. Farewell, dear Miss Perry, and with much love
believe me,

> Yours most sincerely,
> Mimi.

From the above, it would appear that Madeleine had communicated the sad news to Emile personally in some way,
and, since it would probably have been too risky to engineer a meeting, it is most likely that she wrote to him, but
no trace of such a letter has survived. It also appears that
Madeleine had also resigned herself to not seeing Miss
Perry again.

L'Angelier, it would seem, did not take Madeleine's
letter very seriously, and probably thought she was just
'blowing hot and cold'. He sat down and penned a letter to
her which read in part:

> 10 Bothwell-street, Glasgow
> 19 July 1855

[no salutation]

I did not deserve to be treated as you have done. How you
astonish me by writing such a note without condescending to
explain the reasons why your father refuses his consent. He
must have reasons . . . Never, dear Madeleine, could I have
believed you were capable of such conduct. I believed you true
to your word and to your *honour*. What would you think if even
one of your servants had played with anyone's affections as
you have done?

You have deceived your father as you have deceived me.
You never told him how solemnly you bound yourself to me,
or if you had, for the honour of his daughter he could not have
asked [you] to break off an engagement as yours. Think what
your father would say if I sent him your letters for a perusal. Do
you think he could sanction your breaking your promises?

I flatter myself he can only accuse me of a want of for-
tune . . .

The letter was unsigned. But it had the desired effect,
though less from the veiled hint of blackmail than from the
appeal to her conscience. He was genuinely in love with
Madeleine, but he wanted to be accepted as an equal by her
family, across the barriers of class and nationality.

Madeleine was, of course, much more in a position to realize that this would be impossible, in the climate of the *mores* of the mid-nineteenth century.

The family returned to Rowaleyn once more and Madeleine was soon engaged in manoeuvring opportunities to meet her lover again. She, too, was in love with Emile – not just 'in love with love' as they say. She would otherwise never have surrendered herself so utterly and completely. And, by the same token, she harboured a hope, albeit a somewhat desperate one, that somehow, some day, they would be able to marry, despite parental objections. But how? and when?

On returning to Rowaleyn Madeleine lost no time in enlisting her personal maid, Christina Haggart, as an accomplice, enabling her to receive L'Angelier at home while her parents were on holiday with their other children, leaving Madeleine in charge as housekeeper. Then, of course, when her parents and siblings were in residence, there was always the ever obliging Miss Perry who, predictably, had told L'Angelier a few months previously, 'She will be back, mark my words.'

On 3 December 1855 Madeleine sent the following missive to her lover from Glasgow. I have shortened it considerably.

> My own darling husband,
>   I did not expect the pleasure of seeing you last evening, my sweet one, or of being *fondled* by you, dear, dear Emile. Cook was ill and went to bed at 10 – that was the reason I could see you, sweet one of my soul, my love, my all, my own best beloved . . . My beloved, will we require to be married in E. [Edinburgh] or will it do here? You know I know nothing of these things. I fear the Banns in Glasgow, there are so many people know me. But we must manage in some way to be united ere we leave town . . .
>   Much, much love, kisses, tender, long embraces, kisses, love. I am thy own, thy ever fond, thy own dear loving, thy
>   Mimi L'Angelier.

Further effusions in similar vein followed in increasingly rapid succession, including a special letter to Emile on the

occasion of his birthday, 29 April 1856. She wished him
many happy returns, in the traditional manner, but he was
destined never to have another birthday to celebrate . . .

By this time, the Smith family was once again at Rowaleyn, and Madeleine could meet Emile only occasionally in
the garden, with her maid acting as look-out. She also
arranged for letters to be sent to her care of the local
post-office, under the name of 'Miss Bruce', which her maid
Christina Haggart collected. After one such meeting in the
garden, Madeleine was moved to write:

> My own, my beloved husband,
>   Thank you, my love, for coming so far to see your Mimi.
> Beloved, if we did wrong last night, it was in the excitement of
> our love. Yes, beloved, I did truly love you with my soul. I was
> happy . . . Oh, if we could have remained, never more to be
> parted. But we must hope that the time shall come. Darling, I
> love you. Yes, my own Emile, I love you with my heart and
> soul. Am I not your wife? And you may rest assured after what
> has passed I cannot be the wife of any other. No, now it would
> be a sin . . .
>   Adieu again, my husband. God bless you, and may you yet
> be very happy with your Mimi as your little wife. Kindest love,
> fond embrace and kisses from thy own true and ever devoted,
> thy faithful
>
>   Mimi.

L'Angelier replied to this letter with a long epistle. 'My
dearest and beloved wife,' he wrote, 'I got home quite
safely after leaving you.' Then, after this somewhat (for
him) prosaic start, he reverted to his more usual style,
blended with a curious streak of puritanism:

> Though we have sinned, ask earnestly God's forgiveness and
> blessings that all the obstacles in our way may be removed
> from us . . . I am sad at what we did – I regret it very much.
> Think of the consequences if I were never to marry you. Mimi,
> unless Huggins [his employer] helps me I cannot see how I
> shall be able to marry you for years. It is your parents' fault if
> shame is the result; they are to blame for it all. Do speak to your
> brother, open your heart to him, and try to win his friendship.
> Tell him if he loves you to take your part. Speak to your

mother. Tell her . . . that you cannot be the wife of anyone else than me. Tell them you are my wife before God. Do not let them leave you without being married, for I cannot answer what would happen. My conscience reproaches me for a sin that marriage only can efface. I dread lest some great obstacle prevents our marriage . . .

From the above it is clear that L'Angelier was no shallow seducer but a man in whom the urgent passions of youth were tempered by religious scruples and a solicitude for the woman of his choice. He was not known to have philandered with other women, at least not during the period of his affair with Madeleine Smith. Other letters in existence reveal that on several occasions during their meetings both parties strove valiantly to control their physical passions, and on those occasions when they failed they expressed remorse at having given way to sin. It should be noted that such expressions of remorse were far more frequently voiced by L'Angelier than by Madeleine. It seemed that, while she did not actively try to break down her lover's resistance, she did not seem to share his guilty feelings to the same extent.

The time came when L'Angelier persuaded Huggins to raise his salary, with more success than he had dared to hope – his employer doubled it to one pound a week at a stroke. He wrote exultant letters to Madeleine, enthusiastically formulating plans for marriage. 'I will speak to Huggins in September,' he wrote, 'for time to set our marriage.' He did not elaborate which year the September would be. But he made it clear that marriage was his object; this was no casual affair.

In the mean time, although Madeleine's parents had no inkling that she was still meeting her lover (Madeleine having covered her tracks very successfully), the pater-familias had noticed Madeleine's complete lack of interest in meeting any young men in her social circle, and this had not gone unremarked. Mr Smith thought it time that a young lady of twenty should start thinking about preparing to find a suitable suitor, and he introduced an eligible Glasgow bachelor, a Mr William Minnoch, who earned

£3,000 a year as a merchant in the city and who moved in
Glasgow society. Mr Smith approved of him highly, and
saw to it that he was able to meet Madeleine as often as
propriety allowed. Her mother, too, liked Mr Minnoch and
would make pointed remarks about what a good husband
he would make for *somebody*.

It was not long before Madeleine herself began to recon-
sider Mr Minnoch in the light of her parents' admonitions,
and to realize that he would make a much better match than
the impoverished Emile. To acquiesce in her parents'
urgings that she should become officially betrothed to the
eligible merchant would also please them very much and
prove to them that she had good judgement after all.
Madeleine did love her parents dearly, and she knew that
she might have to make sacrifices in order to preserve their
esteem.

Madeleine was not prepared, however, to relinquish her
liaison with her lover until such time as she would be
compelled to do so by marrying Mr Minnoch. In this
L'Angelier himself made her situation even more difficult,
since he was quite clearly not prepared to give her up and
was still bent on marrying her as soon as he was in a
position to do so. Time enough, though, to think about
making the break nearer the time – and meanwhile she set
about entering upon a course of duplicity which would
enable her to have her cake and eat it too, as the saying
goes. So the letters and the meetings in the garden
continued.

It was inevitable, of course, that L'Angelier would get to
hear rumour. Madeleine made no secret of the fact that she
had attended dances, concerts and other social functions
with Mr Minnoch as her escort, pointing out that a lady
could not go alone on such occasions, and that her brothers
were not always available to accompany her. She also made
the point that Mr Minnoch was a friend of her father, and
that she would displease him if she refused. 'But,' she
wrote, 'I would not hide that from you. It is only you,
Emile, that I love. You should not mind public report. No
other has a place in my heart. As to Mr Minnoch, he is
Papa's friend, but I have no regard for him. You hear all the

stories and believe them . . . Emile, my own, my ever dear husband, I have suffered much on your account from my family . . .'

L'Angelier replied telling Madeleine that she was far too fond of 'gallivanting about' and that if she considered herself a married woman she should behave like one. He also moved his lodgings – he left the house in the Botanic Gardens for a house owned by a Mrs Jenkins at 11 Franklin Place, which was considerably nearer Blythswood Square. He was perturbed by the fact that Madeleine, owing to her new commitments, was unable to see him so frequently, although the flow of letters continued unabated. In these, he frequently expressed a doubt that the rumours *were* only rumours and that they might have a substantial basis in fact, but Madeleine somehow managed to convince him with devious excuses and, when all else failed, she took incredible risks smuggling him into the house in the dead of night. After one such encounter she wrote:

> My dear Emile,
> Our meeting last-night was peculiar . . . You say I am indifferent because I shall not be able to see you much . . . Our letters I don't see how I am to do. I intended to speak to you of all this last-night, but we were so engaged otherways . . .
> Dearest love of a husband, I am going to bid you good-night. Would you were beside me, and I would fall asleep on your bosom, dearest love. What would I not give to place my head on your breast, kiss and fondle you – and then I am sure you would kindly *love* me . . . if you were here now I am sure I would allow you to *love* me – I could not resist you, my love, my own beloved Emile . . .
> Dearest love, fond embraces, much love and kisses from your devoted wife, your loving and affectionate wife,
> Mimi L'Angelier.

This letter, sent in October 1856, was penned by the same Madeleine who was planning to marry William Minnoch, three months before their official engagement. But her main concern now was to devise a way of keeping up the correspondence without arousing any suspicions on the part of her family. Her problem was to *receive* letters; there was no problem in sending them. She shared a bedroom in the basement of the house with her youngest sister Janet, who, fortunately for Madeleine, was a sound sleeper. The room had two windows, set very low at street level, protected by bars to discourage thieves. Madeleine worked out that Emile could drop a letter behind these bars, and by opening the window at the bottom she could retrieve it. She explained the scheme to her lover thus:

> Sweet love, you should get those brown envelopes – they would not be so much seen as white ones – to put down into my window. You should just stoop to tie your shoe, and then slip it in . . .

Take a letter, Miss Smith!

Miss Smith took, and replied to, a good many letters in the next few weeks. As part of her scheming, her letters to L'Angelier became shorter than usual, and she also deliberately introduced a good many references to the ubiquitous Mr Minnoch, obviously to prepare her lover insidiously for the shock of the forthcoming event. The engagement would without doubt be announced in the society columns of the newspapers, and all she could hope for was that he would somehow fail to read it. A hearsay 'rumour' she could always scotch, but she could hardly discount an official notice. In one letter, sent in mid January 1857, Madeleine wrote: 'Mr. M. dined with us to-night – do you know, I think if you knew him you would like him, he is most kind. I like him very much better than I used to do.' That, surely, must have been the understatement of the year on her part!

Another letter read in part:

> Emile, my own beloved, you have just left me. Oh, sweet darling, at this moment my heart and soul burns [sic] with love for thee, my husband, my own sweet one . . . A dark spot is in the future – what can it be? Oh, God, keep it from us. Oh, may we be happy – dear darling, pray for our happiness. If we could only get married, all would be well.

Five days later Madeleine Smith accepted William Minnoch's formal proposal of marriage, on 28 January 1857.
The Smith family was delighted. But Madeleine could
still not bring herself to break off her association with
L'Angelier. But she did at least attempt to imply in her
letters that her affections were cooling: her double life had,
at a stroke, become so much more fraught with risk that she
deemed it prudent to try to leave herself an escape route:

> Since you are not pleased with the letters I send you, then our
> correspondence shall be at an end . . . I trust to your honour as
> a gentleman that you will not reveal anything that may have
> passed between us. I shall feel obliged by your bring [sic] me
> my letters and Likeness on Thursday-evening at 7 o'clock. Be at
> the area gate, and C.H. [Christina Haggart, her maid] will take
> the parcel from you . . .

The letter was signed simply 'M'. Emile did not reply.
   On 9 February she wrote again:

> You may well be astonished at this sudden change, but for
> some time back you must have noticed a coolness in my notes.
> My love for you has ceased, and that is why I was cool. I did
> once love you truly, fondly, but for some time back I have lost
> much of that love. There is no other reason for my conduct . . .
> I did at one time love you with heart and soul. It has cost me
> much to tell you this . . . I know you will never injure that
> character of one you so fondly loved. No, Emile, I know you
> have honour and are a Gentleman. What has passed you will
> not mention. I know when I ask that you will comply. Adieu.

Emile was stung into action. He replied telling Madeleine
that she was his wife before God and that he would show
her letters to her father to prove it. Although Madeleine had
burned most of his letters, he had kept most of hers,
particularly the ones which proved the degree of intimacy
between them. Madeleine was now desperate:

> Monday-night. Emile, I have just had your note. Emile, for the
> love you once had for me, do nothing until I see you – for God's
> sake do not bring your once-loved Mimi to an open shame . . .

When I ceased to love you, believe me, it was not to love another. I am free from all engagements at present. Emile, for God's sake do not send my letters to Papa. On Wednesday-night come to the area gate at 12, and I shall open my shutter . . .'

L'Angelier did not see Madeleine at her window that night, but at some time during the hours of darkness he left a note saying that he would do nothing until he saw her the following night. So at midnight she replied:

Emile, I have this night received your note. Oh, it is kind of you to write to me. Emile, no one can know the intense agony of mind I have suffered . . . Emile, my father's wrath would kill me; you little know his temper . . . I loved you and wrote to you in my first ardent love – it was with my deepest love I loved you . . . I put on paper what I should not. I was free, because I loved you with my heart . . . On my bended knees I write you and ask you, as you hope for mercy at the Judgment, do not make me a public shame.

I did love you, and it was my soul's ambition to be your wife. I have cooled, but it was not love for another, for there is no one I love.

Emile saw Madeleine the following night, for in her next letter she mentioned how glad she was to see him looking so well, though this might have been difficult at midnight. She asked him to return her letters, and excused the brief-ness of her note by saying she had cut a finger of her right hand.

On Thursday, 19 February, the ever solicitous Mr Minnoch accompanied Madeleine to the opera where *Lucrezia Borgia* was showing. One is forced to conjecture whether this opera had inspired Madeleine, in the light of subsequent events . . .

A brief entry in L'Angelier's diary for that date confirms that he saw 'Mimi' for a few moments after she returned from her night out. He also notes that he was 'very ill during the night'. After recovering from the bilious attack, he went the next day to a doctor, who prescribed 'physic' which seemed to clear up the symptoms to the extent that the very next day he was able (according to his diary entry) to spend two hours with 'M'. It seemed that passion had won the day, and a great reconciliation had taken place, most probably in Christina Haggart's room after the maid had discreetly withdrawn. That such a reconciliation had come about was amply confirmed by Madeleine's next letter:

> Dearest, sweet Emile,
> I am sorry to hear you have been ill. I hope to God you will soon be better. Take care of yourself – do not go to the office this-week, just stay at home till Monday. Sweet love, it will please me to hear you are well. I have not felt very well these last two days . . . Everyone is complaining: it must be something in the air . . .
> You did look bad Sunday-night and Monday-morning . . . I am longing to meet again, sweet love. We shall be so happy . . . Adieu, my love, my pet, my sweet Emile. A fond, dear tender love and sweet embrace. Ever with love,
> Yours,
> Mimi.

This letter, from a young lady who only the previous Saturday had purchased six pennyworth of arsenic from Murdoch Brothers, the druggists, in Sauchiehall Street 'to be used in our country garden to kill weeds', must surely take the biscuit. George Murdoch, who knew Madeleine, asked her to sign the book, and he duly handed over one ounce of arsenic – enough to kill a hundred men.

On 2 March L'Angelier went to tea with Miss Perry and she commented on how ill he looked. 'I was so ill,' he said, 'that I never expected to see you again.' He told her of his violent bout of sickness on 19 February, and said that he had not felt really completely well since. Asked what he thought had caused it, he said that he attributed it to a cup of cocoa he had taken that night. He did not say where he had it.

On the following Monday, in the early hours of the morning, L'Angelier rang the bell in his room to summon his landlady, Mrs Jenkins. As she rushed upstairs she could hear him vomiting, and when she entered his room he told her that he had a raging thirst and was shivering with cold despite the numerous blankets and quilt on his bed. He also complained of violent stomach and bowel pains. Mrs Jenkins sent her other lodger for a doctor, and also sent him with a message to inform Mr Huggins that Emile was too sick to go in to the office that day.

After his recovery he wrote to Madeleine, explaining why he had been unable to see her at her window, or even drop her a letter behind the bars. He also took her to task regarding the reports he was hearing that she was to be married to another.

Mimi dear, [he wrote]
   Mrs. Anderson surely would not say that your mother told her things when she had not . . . Place yourself in my position and tell me I am wrong in believing what I hear . . . Mimi, I *insist* on having an answer to the questions you evaded in my last. If you evade answering them this time, I must try some other means of coming to the truth. If not answered in a satisfactory manner, you must not expect I shall again write you personally or meet you . . . Who gave you the trinket you were wearing? Is it true it was Mr. Minnoch? And is it true that you are, directly or indirectly, engaged to Mr. Minnoch or to anyone else but me? These questions I must know . . . I will wait to hear from you. I hope nothing will happen to check the happiness we were again enjoying. May God bless you, and with many fond and tender embraces, believe me with kind love, your ever affectionate husband,
                    Emile L'Angelier.

On 12 March Madeleine and William Minnoch set the date for their wedding on 18 June. The same day saw her pen a letter to her lover which ran in part:

My sweet, dear pet,
   I am so sorry you should be so vexed. Believe no reports, sweet one, unless I tell you myself. These rumours have been six months spoken of. They are but for the love of talking, by those who have nothing to do. Even B. [Bessie] has to put up with the same kind of thing. It is true that I went to Mr. Minnoch's house, but I was sent a message by my father because he could not go himself. I will tell and answer all your

questions when we meet. Adieu, dearest love of my soul – with fond and tender embraces, ever believe me, with love and kisses, to be your own fond, dear and loving
Mimi.

On 21 March Mrs Jenkins saw her lodger leaving at about 9 p.m. He was later seen at various times in the city, looking as though he were loitering to pass the time, like a man who was too early for an appointment. Later he called at a lodging-house and asked to see a friend who lived there, but he was out. The place was less than five minutes' walk from Blythswood Square.

There is no written record of where L'Angelier spent the next few hours, though conjecture is not difficult. What we do know is that at 2.30 a.m. Mrs Jenkins was awakened by the violent ringing of the doorbell. Hastily throwing on some clothes and slippers, she opened the door. L'Angelier, bent almost double, was crouched on the doorstep, clutching his stomach in agony. 'I'm very bad,' he said. 'Help me, please.'

Mrs Jenkins somehow got him up the stairs and into his room, and placed the chamber-pot before him as by this time he was vomiting uncontrollably. 'I thought I would never get home,' he gasped; 'I was so bad along the road.' He again complained of a raging thirst, and Mrs Jenkins brought him a full tumbler of water, which he drank at a gulp. She then went off to make a pot of tea.

On returning with the tea, L'Angelier had half undressed and was lying on the bed, obviously very ill indeed. Again he complained of feeling cold, and she put stone hot-water bottles to his stomach and feet and brought more blankets. At seven o'clock, seeing no improvement, she went for the doctor.

'What do you think it is?' he inquired.

Mrs Jenkins shook her head. 'I have no idea. Something internal, obviously. It's strange, though. This is the third time he has gone out well and come back very ill. I must speak to him and ask the cause.'

The doctor left, saying he would be back between ten and eleven o'clock. Mrs Jenkins went back to the sick man.

'What do you think has brought this on?' she asked.

'I had a cup of coffee or cocoa, I can't remember which,' he replied.

'Who gave it to you?'

'My intended,' he replied.

At about nine o'clock Mrs Jenkins went into his room again to draw the curtains, and in the morning light she could see that her lodger was very ill indeed. He lay drenched with sweat, and the chamber-pot was full to the brim with greenish vomit. She asked him if there was anyone he wished to see, and he replied that he would like Miss Perry to come. Mrs Jenkins sent her little boy to fetch her from her house at 144 Renfrew Street. In the mean time Mrs Jenkins kept looking in to see that her patient was as comfortable as possible. 'If only I could sleep for five minutes,' he said, 'I think I would get better.'

The doctor called at the appointed time. 'I think he is asleep now,' she told him, having just looked in on him. 'It would be a pity to waken him now.'

The doctor went in and took the patient's pulse. 'He is dead, madam,' he said simply.

Miss Perry arrived, and was told she had arrived just a few moments too late. Since L'Angelier had asked for her, Mrs Jenkins had naturally assumed that Miss Perry was the woman he was hoping to marry. She was visibly shocked when this old lady in her seventies announced her identity.

'You are not the intended, ma'am?' she inquired timidly.

'Oh, no! I am only a friend.'

'I heard he was going to be married,' Mrs Jenkins said, trying valiantly to recover her composure. 'How shocked and sorry the lady will be.'

Miss Perry broke down in tears. 'I will have to tell her myself,' she sobbed, kissing the dead man's forehead.

After L'Angelier's body had been laid out, his regular doctor arrived, together with his fellow lodger, and William A. Stevenson, a fellow employee from Messrs Huggins' office. Mrs Jenkins then looked through L'Angelier's clothes, which had been thrown carelessly on the sofa. In one pocket was a letter, which she handed to Stevenson. After perusing it he handed it to Miss Perry, who had stayed at the house. The letter – Madeleine's last to her lover – read:

> [no salutation]   [undated]
>   Why, my beloved, did you not come to me? Oh, beloved, are you ill? Come to me, sweet one. I waited and waited for you, but you came not. I shall wait again to-morrow-night, same hour and arrangement. Do come, sweet love, my own dear love of a sweetheart. Come, beloved, and clasp me to your heart. Come, and we shall be happy. A kiss, fond love. Adieu with tender embraces, ever believed me to be your own ever dear fond
>
>   Mimi.

No offer of a cup of cocoa here – the last one had done its job.

Miss Perry visited the house at 7 Blythswood Square, which she had never been to before, to tell Madeleine about the death of her lover. It was said that she took this very calmly – much too calmly, Miss Perry thought, for a woman who had written the letter found in L'Angelier's pocket . . .

The next day saw the post-mortem being carried out by Dr Thomson and Dr Steven, who were not satisfied as to the cause of death. Apart from the unusual character of the symptoms, it was incredible that a healthy and virile young man of thirty should die so suddenly. Then there was the strange coincidence which had aroused the doctors' suspicions: L'Angelier had had three bouts of illness all following the consumption of a cup of coffee or cocoa. The findings of the post-mortem were made known on the Saturday of that week: they had found almost 84 grains of arsenic in L'Angelier's body – enough to kill forty men.

That afternoon Madeleine Smith was arrested and charged with the murder of Emile L'Angelier by poison.

The nine-day trial opened on Tuesday, 30 June 1857, in the Edinburgh High Court of Justiciary, before three judges, the Lord Justice-Clerk (Lord Hope), Lord Ivory and Lord Handyside. The Lord Advocate (Lord Moncrieff) and the Solicitor-General (Mr Maitland) appeared for the Crown; Madeleine Smith was defended by the Dean of

Faculty (Mr Inglis), Mr George Young and Mr Alexander Moncrieff (no relation to Lord Moncrieff).

The court was crammed to capacity, all seats having been taken two hours before the proceedings opened. The charge against the prisoner at the bar was that firstly on two separate occasions in February 1857 she administered arsenic or other poison to Pierre Emile L'Angelier with intent to murder him, and that secondly on an occasion in March 1857, by means of poison, she murdered the said L'Angelier. To both charges she pleaded not guilty in an audible subdued voice.

The jury of fifteen men all came from Edinburgh or its immediate environs, and comprised three farmers, a merchant, two shoemakers, a currier, a clerk, a cabinetmaker, a cowman, a teacher and four gentlemen of independent means.

The Lord Advocate called fifty-seven witnesses for the prosecution; the dice seemed loaded against the unhappy Madeleine Smith from the start. Mrs Jenkins described how L'Angelier had died in agony; Miss Perry told how she hastened to the house to see him but was a few minutes too late – one wonders whether, if she had arrived sooner, L'Angelier might have confided to her, on his death-bed, the suspicions he must have had about the coffee or cocoa he had received from the hand of his intended. His colleague at Messrs Huggins', William Stevenson, told of searching the dead man's office desk, where 198 letters from Madeleine were found, which combined with the ones found in his lodgings made a total of more than 300. It was these letters – some of them in particular – which were to cause such a sensation at this trial. The Lord Advocate was at great pains to impugn Madeleine's character by quoting from those letters which he allowed to be put into evidence. Many were considered too improper to be read out in court, and only sixty of the letters were read.

The Dean of Faculty referred to the letters as 'this frightful correspondence', but it was the Lord Justice-Clerk who really went to town in his scathing comments. He referred to Madeleine's habit of underscoring the word 'love' with three lines in such sentences as 'I am sure I would allow you to *love* me', pointing out that this was simply a euphemism for sexual intercourse. He referred to other letters in which veiled yet obvious references were made to her having lost her virginity to L'Angelier and to some confusion as to the date of her anticipated period and her fear of pregnancy. 'These letters', the Lord Justice-Clerk continued, 'show as extraordinary a frame of mind and as unhallowed a passion as perhaps ever appeared in a court of justice.' Referring to a particular letter dated 7 May 1856, he said: 'It is the letter of a girl rejoicing in what had passed, and alluding to it, in one passage in particular, in terms which I will not read, for perhaps they were never previously committed to paper as having passed between a man and a woman . . . Certainly such a sentence was probably never before penned by a female to a man.' This last statement very clearly demonstrates the standards of morality and propriety expected of women at the time.

The forensic evidence of the doctors who had performed the autopsy of L'Angelier's body gave long and highly technical descriptions of their findings. A large number of gruesome-looking exhibits were shown, such as glass bottles containing portions of the unfortunate L'Angelier's stomach, liver, intestines, lungs and heart, and phials of various liquids extracted from these organs. These were passed round for examination by the fifteen good men and true, who looked at them without batting an eyelid. It is unlikely that the shoemakers, the cabinetmaker or the currier even knew what the doctors in the witness-box were talking about, and whether the four gentlemen of independent means had ever studied toxicology in their leisure is open to question.

Madeleine's own statement was read out in court. At that time a defendant was not permitted to give evidence personally, but it is interesting to speculate what the result might have been had she been allowed to go into the witness-box. One inevitably wonders how she would have reacted to one particular question which the prosecution would without doubt have asked her: why she wrote her last passionate appeal to her lover to come to her. It must be remembered that at this time preparations were going

ahead for her impending marriage to William Minnoch, so
she must have been desperately thrashing about for some
means of disposing of the lover who by now had become an
acute embarrassment. She could scarcely have denied that
this was indeed the position in which she found herself.

The question of why Madeleine purchased arsenic was
hotly debated by both sides. She maintained that she had
wanted it to use as a cosmetic preparation, and the defence
cited several instances of its use for such purposes in
literature. Madeleine also said that a girl she had known at
school had recommended it, but when this girl, now a
married woman, was traced and put up as a witness by the
prosecution, she averred that she had told Madeleine
nothing of the kind, adding, 'She must have read it in a
book.' Much was also made of the fact that Madeleine had
told the chemist that she wanted the poison to kill weeds in
the garden of Rowaleyn, and it was pointed out that
although the gardeners used weedkilling materials they did
not have authority to purchase them, which was the re-
sponsibility of Mr Smith and not Madeleine, and that Mr
Smith would not have entrusted his daughter to purchase
them, especially since he was quite easily able to do so
himself. Madeleine's reply to this was to say that she had
told the chemist that it was for killing weeds rather than
saying it was for cosmetic use, because she thought that
they would not have supplied it to her otherwise. An
interesting point crops up here: Madeleine charged the
arsenic to her father's account!

Two doctors gave evidence that, on the basis of such
reports as they had read about the cosmetic uses of arsenic,
they had washed their hands and faces in a solution of
arsenic in water, to see if their complexion would be improved and the skin of their hands whitened, without ill
results. The Lord Advocate replied drily that as yet it might
be too soon to look for results of any kind . . .

The Dean of Faculty made a brilliant speech. He pulled
out all the stops, depicting Madeleine as a pure and innocent maiden seduced and blackmailed by the dastardly
L'Angelier – both of which descriptions are far from the
truth. Madeleine, as will quickly be seen from a perusal of

her letters, made quite a lot, if not all, of the running, and
L'Angelier was driven more by human passion than any
other emotion. This is amply demonstrated in an encounter
he had in the office one morning with Thomas Fleming
Kennedy, the cashier at Messrs Huggins', who testified
that L'Angelier had come to him weeping, saying that
Madeleine wished to break off their engagement. Mr
Kennedy had replied that the lady was not worthy of him
and that he should return her letters, to which L'Angelier
had replied, 'No, I won't – she shall never marry another
man as long as I live.' Does that sound like the utterance of a
man intending to blackmail his mistress? In my view, he
wished to keep the letters to use as a last resort – to show
her father if that gentleman were to put any serious impedi-
ment in the way of their marriage at some future date – for
example, if he should try to block their wedding plans even
after Madeleine attained her majority the following year,
or, possibly, if she should inadvertently become pregnant.
Mr Smith, with proof in his hands of how far their liaison
had progressed, could then scarcely refuse. His honour as a
gentleman, L'Angelier considered, would surely override
any of his class or other social prejudices.

A grocer, originally from Jersey, was found who had
shared a room with L'Angelier at the Rainbow Tavern in
Edinburgh in 1852. He had continued to meet his compat-
riot as a drinking companion up to L'Angelier's death. On
one occasion in 1857, the grocer said, L'Angelier had told
him that he was fed up with life. 'I never was so unhappy in
my whole existence,' he had said. 'I wish I had the courage
to blow my brains out.' The witness could not remember
the date on which this encounter took place, but it would
seem, on the face of it, that it must have been shortly after
one of Madeleine's periodic rebuffs, when L'Angelier
would most likely have taken refuge in an alcoholic binge.

A reaction of this kind is more likely to be experienced by
a man desperately in love and suffering the humiliation of
being the target of a fiancée playing hard to get – even
allowing for the Gallic temperament which he undoubtedly
had in fair measure. It certainly does not sound like the
behaviour of a ruthless blackmailer. But, however suicidal

he might feel, no one in his right mind would kill himself by taking arsenic, as the defence tried to imply. Compared to other poisons, arsenic kills slowly, and death would, as we have seen, be preceded by vomiting, diarrhoea, weakness, cold tremors and excruciating pains in the stomach and bowels. I venture to submit that no one in his right mind would kill himself anyway – but that is by the way.

The Lord Advocate, on the seventh day of the trial, spoke from ten in the morning until half-past three in the afternoon. His peroration was fair, but its main weak point was that he was unable to prove conclusively that Madeleine and L'Angelier had met on the nights preceding those occasions when he was taken ill. At the close of the Lord Advocate's speech the court was adjourned until the following day.

The eighth day of the trial opened at ten o'clock with the impassioned speech of the Dean of Faculty taking up most of the day, and after an interval of fifteen minutes, towards the end of the afternoon the Lord Chief Justice-Clerk began his summing-up. Having, during the trial, heard fifty-seven witnesses for the prosecution and thirty-two for the defence, as well as the long speeches of his fellow judges, Lord Hope, who was sixty-three at the time, declared that he was too exhausted to complete it that night, and adjourned the trial once more, so that it now went into its ninth day.

The summing-up was fair and unbiased, and warned the jury of the dangers of inferring too much from circumstantial evidence.

You must bear in mind [Lord Hope said] that arsenic could have been administered by [the accused] only if she had a meeting with L'Angelier, and this meeting would have to be proved to have taken place, without any shadow of doubt . . . It would also have to be proved beyond any reasonable doubt that she had met L'Angelier immediately prior to his having been stricken by the symptoms of arsenical poisoning on each of the three occasions, the first two with regard to the charge of attempted murder, and the last and fatal occasion as relating to the charge of murder . . . Gentlemen of the jury, the fact that L'Angelier was seen in the vicinity of the accused's house

between nine and eleven o'clock on the night before his death,
whatever you may infer from this, is still no proof that a cup of
cocoa containing arsenic, prepared by the accused, ever
touched his lips.

At ten minutes past one the jury retired. They took only 22
minutes to reach their tripartite verdict. They elected their
teacher juryman, Mr Moffat of Edinburgh High School, to
be their foreman and to read out their findings: not guilty,
by a majority, of the first charge of administering poison
with intent to murder; not proven, by a majority, on the
second charge; and not proven, again by a majority, on the
third charge of murder by means of poison. 'Not proven' is,
of course, a peculiar to Scottish law. This is a pity, because it
is a very appropriate verdict to cover a case beset by
elements of doubt, as so many are.

The prisoner at the bar was then granted an 'assoilzie' – a
quaint Scottish term meaning an acquittal. It derives from
the archaic verb 'assoil', meaning to pardon, but is still used
in legal terminology.

Madeleine was cheered and congratulated as she left the
court. Four days later, she wrote a letter to Miss Aitken, the
matron at Edinburgh Prison, thanking her for her care and
consideration while she had been there, and asking her to
forward her Bible and watch to her brother.

The trial had ruined the Smith family socially. They left
Glasgow and moved, first to Bridge of Allan and later to
Polmont. James Smith continued with his architectural
consultancy, though fewer clients came; his wife remained
an invalid and spent more time in bed than out of it. Bessie
and Janet never married.

As to Madeleine, she never saw William Minnoch again,
much less married him. Her brother took her to London,
and from there, at the end of 1857, she went to Plymouth to
live in the house of a clergyman. In the New Year she met a
young art teacher named George J. Wardle at a class in
watercolour painting which she attended. Wardle later
obtained a position with William Morris's decorating and
furnishing business, and he and Madeleine were married at
St Paul's, the parish church of Knightsbridge, on 4 July

1861. Her father travelled from Polmont to give her away, though his thoughts on that occasion are not on record. Wedding guests, however, reputedly referred to him as a melancholy man. He returned to Polmont afterwards, where he died two years later.

The Wardles settled in Bloomsbury and Madeleine became a leading light in the social circle associated with the William Morris and Socialist Society. She met William Morris, and became a renowned hostess. She also became manageress of the Central Democratic Club, of which George Bernard Shaw was a member. Shaw received coffee at Madeleine's hands, and lived for more than seventy years afterwards.

The Wardles had two children, but their family happiness was not to last beyond 1889, when George Wardle left William Morris's employ on health grounds and emigrated to Italy, leaving his wife in London. They did not meet again. Wardle died in 1910.

At the age of eighty Madeleine decided to emigrate to the United States, where her son Thomas was then living. Madeleine, although she had long ago discarded the notion that arsenic was good for the complexion, looked twenty years younger than her age, and an elderly Roman Catholic Irish-American named Sheehy proposed to her and was accepted. Marriage certainly seemed to suit her. This one lasted until her death in New York on 12 April 1928, at the age of ninety-two.

Yes, Madeleine Smith, or Wardle, or Sheehy, remained an inveterate romantic until the end. One inevitably wonders whether the happiness she craved would have lasted a lifetime had she married Emile L'Angelier. I have no ideas on the subject myself; but then I am not a romantic.

5

The Triangle of Death

Edith Thompson and Frederick Bywaters (1922)

Letters played a very important part in the drama of Edith Thompson, who was accused of inciting her lover, Frederick Bywaters, to murder her husband. Amazingly, the obvious references in her letters to 'having tried ground glass in his food, but it was no good' and to requests to send her some 'powder', adding, almost as an afterthought, 'to see if that will do the job', and finally asking him 'to think of something, as everything I have thought of has had no effect', were dismissed, in the final analysis, by her counsel as so much hot air. 'The imaginings of a feverish mind' was the description given to these references by no less distinguished a counsel than Sir Henry Curtis Bennett, KC!

But we must start this story at the beginning – the trial will come later.

Edith Graydon was twenty-two when she married Percy Thompson on 15 January 1915. In many popular accounts of this case her husband's age is adroitly side-stepped so as to give the impression that Edith was married to a much older man, but this was not so. According to the copy of the marriage certificate in the official records, Percy was only four years older, and it is scarcely likely that the official record is wrong.

Percy was certainly pedestrian and plodding, the very epitome of suburban respectability. He was a shipping clerk in a City of London firm at six pounds a week – hardly a soul-uplifting job, even if it was not soul-destroying. Edith, on the other hand, was a born romantic, a dreamer of dreams, in love with love, sensual, attractive. She was employed, first as a book-keeper and eventually as manageress, by a firm of wholesale milliners, Messrs Carlton and Prior, at 168 Aldersgate Street – less than a quarter of a mile from the Old Bailey to which, a bare seven years later, her passion for a younger man would lead her.

During the seven years of the marriage, the couple lived in Ilford, where in July 1920 they purchased a terraced house at 41 Kensington Gardens. The old lady who sold them the house remained there as a lodger, and the Thompsons also took other lodgers to help pay the mortgage. They commuted to their jobs at about 8.15 a.m. every morning on weekdays and, except when going to the threatre or out to dinner with friends afterwards, they would return home at about 6.45 p.m. They did not have a car; public transport was used for commuting.

This somewhat narrow and commonplace life, bounded by the regularity of routine, irked the romantic Edith, who lived two lives: in one, she was the woman who sat at a desk keeping accounts and travelled back and forth in London's busy streets of commerce; in the other, she was the weaver of fantasies, the heroine of her own tales of wonder and imagination. Her one escape was the reading of romantic fiction; today she would have been one of Mills and Boon's greatest devotees, but there was still plenty of romantic fiction available in her own time: reprints of Victorian classics, contemporary modern love stories, travel and adventure in exotic far-flung places, love on sun-drenched beaches, love on board ship during a cruise, love in the Alpine snows – but always love. It is apparent that the disparity between Edith and her ill-matched spouse showed itself early in the marriage, for they occupied separate rooms after the first few months. There are any number of reasons why Percy was unable to give his wife the love she craved, and the only respectable way in which she could try to assuage her craving was to read romantic fiction. If she had ever toyed with the idea of taking a lover, she had certainly never done anything about it. Until the fateful day when Frederick Bywaters entered her life.

Frederick Bywaters was good-looking, virile and widely travelled. He had a steady job and a personable line of chat for one so young: he was barely eighteen at the time he enters our story. Previously he had attended the same school as Edith's younger brothers and her sister, Avis Graydon. After leaving school, Freddy, as he was known, obtained a position as a ship's clerk on the ss *Morea*. He enjoyed his work, which took him all over the world.

On 4 June 1921 Freddy returned from a four-month voyage to Australia, and was invited by the Graydon family to join them for a one-week holiday on the Isle of Wight. It was on this occasion that he first met Edith and her husband Percy. Edith was able to escape from her husband's chaperonage from time to time and join the other young folks, her brothers, sister and their friends – and Freddy. They had fun, they swam, they played tennis, they flirted – and Edith and Freddy exchanged their first kiss, probably more from bravado than the underlying mutual attraction which was undoubtedly there, if only subconsciously at that stage. A year later Edith was writing to Freddy: 'One year ago to-day we went for that memorable ride round the island in the char-a-banc – do you remember? That was the first time you kissed me.'

At the end of the holiday Percy, who liked the young fellow, invited him to live with them as their lodger, most probably so that he could be nearer his friends the Graydons. Meanwhile the spark of mutual attraction between Edith and Freddy ignited the passion that, like a spreading forest fire, was eventually to consume and destroy them.

On 18 June the holiday ended, with the new lodger wasting no time in moving into the Thompson family home. Only two days later, Edith was already calling him 'darling' and declaring her love for him when he asked her why she was in pensive mood. Friday, 27 June, was Freddy's nineteenth birthday, and the two met for lunch at the Holborn Restaurant. Edith regaled him with an account of how unhappy she was with her husband. 'Let me be a pal to you,' Freddy told her, 'and I will help you if I can.'

A month passed with Percy apparently oblivious to the relationship that was steadily developing between his wife and the personable young man he had taken under his roof. It is said that there are none so blind as those who will not see . . . The Thompsons had been married for six years, and later, at the trial, Edith was to aver that 'she had never been really happy with her husband' and that she had suggested first a separation, then a divorce, long before Bywaters joined the household, but that Percy had refused.

On Monday, 1 August, this subject came up again following an argument during which Percy Thompson hit his wife and abused her, throwing her across a room and bruising her arm. Bywaters was in the garden and saw what was happening through the window, and he rushed into the house and came between Percy and his wife in order to separate them. Afterwards there was a somewhat heated discussion between the three of them, in which Percy accused Bywaters of having more than a normal friendly interest in his wife and told him in no uncertain terms to leave. Edith, for her part, asked her husband once again for a divorce, or at least a separation, and once again he refused. Bywaters told Percy that he should divorce his wife as he knew that she was not happy with him. Percy retorted that he should not interfere, adding, 'She is my wife – I have her and I intend to keep her.'

Four days later Bywaters left the Thompson home and moved into his mother's house in Westow Road, Upper Norwood – a long way from Ilford. But he continued to meet Edith, and it was the correspondence they kept up which was to play so large a part at the subsequent trial. She signed all her letters with the pet name Freddy called her – Peidi (an anglicized form of the Greek word for 'child', which, on the face of it, was a strange name for a woman older than himself).

On 9 September Bywaters sailed on the ss *Morea*, this time bound for the Mediterranean. Over the following year Edith wrote him more than sixty letters; during this time he made five cruises on his ship. Edith wrote to him almost every day while he was on these voyages, receiving his replies at her office. Many of her letters were very long, running on like a diary with numerous anecdotes and gossip, chat about mutual friends and relatives, outings, books she had read and so on. Often she enclosed newspaper and magazine cuttings that she thought would be of interest. She also sent him books she had read with a request that he read them too and subsequently discuss them with her during the course of their correspondence. It was certainly true that this was no mere physical affair: the couple shared many intellectual interests. Later, when her husband started to suspect that she was receiving letters from Bywaters at her office, she used a poste-restante address in the name of 'Miss P. Fisher' at Aldersgate post office.

The letters Edith wrote to her lover began to take a sinister turn from about February 1922. They are admittedly ambiguous in their references, though these were not always as discreetly veiled as they could have been. Look at this example, dated 10 February:

> You must do something . . . opportunities come and go – they have to, because I'm helpless and I think and think and think . . . It would be so easy, darlint, if I had things – I do hope I shall. I have enclosed cuttings of Dr. Wallis's case. It might prove interesting . . .

The cuttings, from the *Daily Sketch* of 9 February 1922, were headed MYSTERY OF CURATE'S DEATH. The curate had been poisoned with hyoscine (the same poison that Crippen used). Another cutting was headed POISONED CHOCOLATES FOR UNIVERSITY CHIEF and subtitled 'Deadly Powder posted to Oxford Chancellor – Ground Glass in Box'. The implication was that Edith wished Freddy to provide her with some kind of toxic substance in order to poison her husband, and this was made much of at the trial.

On 22 February her letter read in part:

> I do hate this life I lead – I hate the lies, and I tell so many that it hurts. If only I could make an absolutely clean, fresh start . . . Darlingest boy, this thing that I am going to do for both of us – will it ever make any difference between us? Darlint, do you understand what I mean? Will you ever think any the less of me? – because of this thing that I shall do. Darlint, if I thought you would, I'd not do it.

The prosecution had a field-day with this one.

The letter Edith wrote on 14 March continued the theme:

> Will you do all the thinking and planning for me, darlint? – for
> this thing – be ready with every little detail when I see you –
> because you know more about this thing than I, and I am
> relying on you for all plans and instructions . . .

What is that if not incitement to murder, thundered the
prosecution after this letter had been read out. And it can
better be conjectured than described what the prosecution's reaction was to the following, dated 1 April:

> He said . . . the tea tasted bitter, as if something had been put
> in it. Now I think whatever else I try it will again taste bitter – he
> will recognise it and be more suspicious still. I'm going to try
> the glass again occasionally . . . I've got an electric light globe
> this time.

The mind boggles. 'Who,' boomed Edith's counsel, the
redoubtable Curtis Bennett, 'would try to poison her husband by putting ground-up electric light bulbs in his tea?
These references are the imaginings of a feverish mind,' he
said, 'fed on a constant diet of cheap romantic fiction!'

The prosecution did not agree . . . and they can scarcely
be blamed after the following excerpt from a letter dated 24
April was read to the court:

> I used the light bulb three times, but the third time he found
> a piece, so I've given up until you come home. I was buoyed
> up with the hope of the light bulb and I used a lot – big pieces,
> too – not powdered, and it has no effect. I quite expected
> to be able to send that cable . . . Oh, darlint, I do feel so down
> and unhappy. Wouldn't the stuff make small pills coated with
> soap and dipped in liquorice powder? You tell me not to leave
> finger marks on the box. Do you know, I did not think of the
> box, but I did think of the glass or cup . . .

In a subsequent letter dated 18 May she quoted from a book
she had been reading about the deadly effects of digitalis if
taken to excess, asking rather naïvely, 'Is it any use?' One
cannot help thinking that, since Bywaters was a ship's clerk

and not a chemist or a doctor, he would hardly be likely to know, and since Edith was intelligent enough to realize this, she was, in this query, appealing to his knowledge as a well-travelled 'man of the world'.

On 14 June she was still harping on the theme of poisoning. 'Darlint,' she wrote, 'how can you get ptomaine poisoning from a tin of salmon? The mother of one of our boys [employees] has died with it.'

Then, later, on 4 July: 'Why aren't you sending me something I wanted you to? . . . if I don't mind the risk, why should you?' Curtis Bennett was barely able to get out of that one by implying that she had meant the risk of detection by her husband if he found any of her lover's clandestine presents! The prosecution took a more down-to-earth view.

Edith's letters, however, were not all couched in this vein. Many were the genuinely sincere outpourings of a woman deeply in love. 'When you have something you've never had before – something you're so happy to have found – you're always afraid of it flying away. That's how I feel about your love – I never want to lose it and live.' She referred to their relationship as 'the Palship of two halves', adding, 'There are two halves in this world who want nothing on earth but to be joined together.'

But on 19 September her words to Freddy implied that he had, at least up to a point, tried somewhat unsuccessfully to break off their relationship:

> Darlingest boy – I don't quite understand you about 'Pals'. You say, 'Can we be Pals only, Peidi, it will make it easier'. Have you lost heart and given up hope? Yes, darlint – you are jealous of *him* – but I want you to be! He has the right by law to all that you have the right to by nature and love – yes, darlint, be jealous – so much that you will do something desperate.

With this letter Edith enclosed a cutting from the *Daily Sketch* headed RAT POISON CONSUMED BY FOWL KILLS WOMAN.

The ss *Morea* docked at Tilbury on 23 September, and Bywaters went straight home to his mother's, making no attempt to see Edith for almost three days. He then met her after work, but only for an hour. It is interesting to speculate what their discussion was about as they lingered over coffee. Did she tell him that to leave her husband, her steady job and her comfortable home would be too much of a sacrifice for her to contemplate? Did he pursue the notion of allowing their relationship to mark time while they tried to sort things out – perhaps another attempt to obtain a divorce? Or did the conversation take a more sinister turn?

It was known that they met at least four times subsequent to this coffee-shop meeting, so any half-hearted decision Bywaters might have made to play down their relationship must have been very short-lived. By 2 October she was writing to him in terms that left no doubt that they had spent a good deal of time in each other's company:

> Darlingest lover of mine – thank you, thank you, oh, thank you a thousand times for Friday – it was lovely . . . And then Saturday – yes, I did feel happy . . . Darlint, we've said we'll always be Pals, haven't we, shall we say we'll always be lovers . . . or is it (this great big love) a thing we can't control? Your love to me is something different, it is my life.

The letter Edith received in reply is one of the only two of Bywaters's letters that survive. Going always as she was in fear of her husband's finding them, she destroyed all the others. Bywaters, on the other hand, had no such inhibitions, and kept all hers. Had he prudently destroyed them – especially the ones containing the references to poison – it is very unlikely that Edith Thompson would have met her fate at the hands of the hangman – a fate which many would say was wholly undeserved, since she did not strike the blow which killed her husband.

There was certainly no hint of playing down the relationship in either of the two extant letters penned by Bywaters, the first undated and probably written on 29 September, the second two days later:

> Darling, Peidi – To-night was impulse – natural – I could not resist – I had to hold you . . . Darlint little girl, I love you so

much, and the only way I can control myself is by not seeing you, and I'm not going to do that! I must have you – I love you, darlint – what others call reason does not enter into our lives . . . Peidi, you are my magnet – I shall never be able to see you and remain impassive.

And on 1 October:

Peidi, I love you more and more every day. It grows, darlint, and will keep on growing . . . I mustn't ever think of losing you. My darlint little girl, I love you more than I will ever be able to show you. Darlint, you are the centre . . .

On the following Tuesday, 3 October, the Thompsons and another couple with whom they were friendly had arranged to go to the Criterion theatre in London's West End. Bywaters knew of this arrangement, and on the night in question he had met Edith after work for a short time, and he left her at Aldersgate Street. To his surprise, Bywaters saw Percy, who had come to meet her. It is not known whether Percy saw his rival, but since Bywaters had not seen Percy for a good many months, it must have been quite a shock. Percy did not normally come to meet his wife after work, and for him to turn up less than five minutes after Bywaters had left her was certainly cutting things a bit close.

Bywaters quickly left and travelled to Manor Park to visit the Graydons, with whom he stayed until 11 p.m. Then he walked to East Ham, but he did not take a train home – he was in too restless a mood. All he could think of was seeing his beloved Peidi. He started walking in the direction of Ilford . . .

Meanwhile, the Thompsons had left the theatre at about 11 p.m., said goodbye to their friends at Piccadilly Circus, and had taken a train on the Tube to Liverpool Street, from where they caught the 11.30 to Ilford. Close to midnight they were walking along Belgrave Road in the direction of the intersection which led to Kensington Gardens, where they lived. Belgrave Road was dark and poorly lit. The couple were chatting amiably, and Edith was trying to persuade Percy to take her to a dance in about a fortnight's time.

Suddenly and without warning a man dressed in an overcoat and hat rushed towards them, pushing Edith Thompson roughly out of his way and grabbing Percy by the lapels of his coat, swinging him round and lunging at him wildly with a knife in his hand. 'You cad!' the assailant shouted. 'You make her life hell! Why don't you divorce her?' Eleven times the knife stabbed, and Percy Thompson slumped to the pavement, sliding down by the wall nearby. One of the wounds had severed the carotid artery in his neck, and within minutes he was dead, suffocated by his own blood.

Edith regained her balance and rushed to the aid of her husband, crying, 'Oh, no! Don't!' but the attacker had already fled. Later Edith was to testify that she had recognized Bywaters, both from his appearance, despite the ill-lit surroundings, and by his voice. 'Someone pushed me,' she stated, 'and I saw my husband scuffling with a man. Then I saw someone running away, and I recognized the coat and hat.' She went to the aid of her husband, who was covered with blood. Seeing that there was nothing she could do, she went to look for a doctor, running along the dark street, sobbing wildly and almost hysterical. She encountered a young couple on their way home from a night out, and begged them to help her. 'Oh, my God!' she cried, 'my husband is bleeding! Will you help me?' They took her to the house of a Dr Maudsley who lived in the vicinity, and pounded on the door until he was awakened. Hastily the doctor threw on some clothes and accompanied his three visitors to the spot where Percy Thompson lay, already beyond all help. They found a local resident, John Webber, standing beside the stricken man, and his wife, striking a match in an effort to see the victim's condition more clearly. It was this man who was later to testify that he had heard a woman's voice cry out 'Oh, no! Don't!' followed by the sound of running feet, and had rushed out to investigate.

At about one o'clock the police arrived, and the body was removed to the mortuary. A Sergeant Mew escorted Mrs Thompson the fifty yards or so to her home, noting a

significant remark she made: 'They'll blame me for this!'
which at the time he attributed to her overwrought state.
Eventually she admitted that the man she had seen running
away from the scene was Bywaters, although at first she
tried to shield him. Later that same night she was taken to
the police station and detained for further questioning,
whereupon she exclaimed: 'Oh, God! Oh, God! What can I
do? Why did he do it? I didn't want him to do it! I must tell
the truth!' She then made a brief statement, in which she
acknowledged that Frederick Bywaters was her husband's
assailant.

Meanwhile, Bywaters's precipitate flight had taken
him, via Wanstead and Leytonstone, in the direction of
Stratford. Running in the shadows, skirting the pools of
lamplight, he dropped the murder weapon down a drain,
and then took a cab to his home, arriving at about 3 a.m.
according to his mother, who heard him come in and
looked at the clock. 'My, but you *are* late!' she called out. In
reply, he told his mother that the last buses had gone and
he had walked most of the way.

On the following day – 4 October – Bywaters thought it
prudent to avoid contacting Edith himself and opted to wait
for her to get in touch with him, little knowing that she was
being detained at the police station to assist the officers with
their inquiries into the death of her husband. In the evening
he paid another visit to the Graydons, his nonchalant
manner doubtless very far removed from his true feelings.
It came, therefore, as a great shock, both to himself and to
the Graydon family, when two police officers called at the
house, told him that he was under arrest for the murder of
Percy Thompson, and took him away to Ilford police
station, where he was formally charged, together with
Edith Thompson. 'Why her?' he replied. 'Mrs Thompson
was not aware of my movements.'

*   *   *

The trial of Edith Thompson and Frederick Bywaters began
on 6 December 1922 before Mr Justice Shearman. Mrs

Thompson was charged not only with murder but with conspiracy to commit murder, incitement to murder and attempted murder. Bywaters was charged with murder only. He was defended by Cecil Whiteley, KC, and Mrs Thompson's counsel was Sir Henry Curtis Bennett, KC. The prosecution was led by the Solicitor-General, Sir Thomas Inskip, assisted by Mr Travers Humphreys, later to become a famous judge. In the event, Mrs Thompson was tried only on the murder indictment. The trial of the two defendants was to last five days.

The Old Bailey has seen a good many trials, but in none was the judge so prejudiced against the female co-defendant as in this one. Mr Justice Shearman took every opportunity he could of pointing out that Edith Thompson was an adulteress. He described her love affair as a 'sordid intrigue' and referred to the undoubtedly sincere expressions of love in her numerous letters in the most deprecating terms – in fact he seemed more concerned with this aspect of the letters than with their references to poisons and the like. Forty-nine letters were put in as exhibits and read to the court, but thirty-four were not allowed in evidence. From my perusal of these letters, it would seem that the main reasons for their omission were firstly, because none of them contained any references to poison, and secondly, some of them contained references to a presumed miscarriage experienced by Mrs Thompson, which her counsel deemed prejudicial to her case. The exclusion of so many of the others was thus aimed at giving undue prominence to the selection of letters describing poisons, ground glass and so on, which would boost the prosecution's case.

Mr Justice Shearman's summing-up searched out all the points in the letters which would throw the most unfavourable light on the female prisoner. Although the greater part of his charge to the jury was biased in the extreme, he did at least point out that only Bywaters's hand struck the fatal blows, although he emphasized his conclusion that there was a clear case of conspiracy between Bywaters and Mr Thompson to murder her husband. This he proceeded to back up with references to the 'poison' and 'ground glass' letters and to the newspaper cuttings enclosed with several of them, which described both accidental and intentional fatal poisonings.

The judge had comparatively little to say about Bywaters, other than that he was a foolish and misguided young man to get himself mixed up with a married woman. He made much more of this relationship than of Bywaters's actual deed stabbing Percy Thompson to death. To this latter point he addresses but few words, emphasizing merely that the deed was done, and seen to be done, and so a *fait accompli* which was the reason why the defendant Bywaters was standing before him in the dock with a charge of murder hanging over him. But why did this murder take place?

'You are told,' the judge continued, 'that this is a case of a great love. A great love! Take one of Mrs Thompson's letters . . . in which she says: "He has the right by law to all that you have the right to by nature and love." Gentlemen, if that . . . means anything, it means that the love of a husband for his wife is something improper because marriage is acknowledged by the law, and that the love of a woman for her lover, illicit and clandestine, is something great and noble. I am certain that you, like any other right-minded persons, will be filled with disgust at such a notion.'

Mr Justice Shearman continued in this vein for most of the remainder of his speech. Clearly he considered this adulterous association to be more reprehensible than killing a man with eleven stab wounds. The knife which Bywaters had discarded had been retrieved by the police, and was shown as an exhibit in court. Significantly, however, the judge made no reference whatever to the findings of Sir Bernard Spilsbury, the pathologist, at the post-mortem, during which not the slightest trace of ground glass, toxic drug or other poisonous substance was found in the deceased's body. Yet he made repeated pointed allusions to the 'conspiracy' element of the murder: 'For months these two people had been corresponding and for months this woman had been writing to this man, inciting him to murder.' A clearer example of brainwashing of a jury by the judge would be hard to find in the annals of British criminal trials.

The result was a foregone conclusion. On 11 December both the accused were found guilty by a unanimous verdict. Asked whether he wished to stay anything, Bywaters replied: 'I say the verdict of the jury is wrong. Edith Thompson is not guilty.' He made no attempt to excuse himself for his part in the crime. After sentence was passed on Edith Thompson, she cried, 'I'm not guilty! Oh God, I'm not guilty!'

Both prisoners appealed, but in both cases the Court of Criminal Appeal upheld the Old Bailey jury's verdict, and on 9 January 1923 Frederick Bywaters was hanged by Pierrepoint at Pentonville at the same time that his mistress went to her fate at the hands of Ellis in Holloway. No notable 'last words' were recorded for either of them, and in the case of Edith Thompson, she had to be drugged and carried in a stupor from her cell to the execution yard. John Ellis, her executioner, retired as hangman a few months later; many people averred that this was the case that broke his nerve. A year or so afterwards, Ellis made an abortive suicide attempt, but recovered. He then took to drink, and seven years later he made another suicide bid, this time successful.

6

The Cyclops Eye

Dr Buck Ruxton (1935)

Imagine that you are on holiday in a scenic area of Scotland and that one day you go for a walk in the bracing air, enjoying the panoramic beauty all around. Coming to a bridge, you see a signpost indicating that this spans a stream known as the Gardenholme Linn. You start walking across the bridge, and when you come to a point somewhere about the middle, you walk to the side and look over the railings into the water.

You note, not without some annoyance, that even here litter-louts have not been idle, and the view of the water running through the ravine under the bridge has been spoiled by someone's having discarded some bundles of rubbish wrapped in newspaper and a sheet or some similar material. Looking more closely, you then see, to your horror, what looks like a human arm protruding from one of the bundles . . .

This is what happened, on Sunday, 29 September 1935, to a Miss Susan Johnson of Edinburgh, who was on holiday at Moffat, a small town on the Edinburgh to Carlisle road. The Gardenholme Linn, which runs into the River Annan, is about two miles north of Moffat, and Miss Johnson never walked two miles more quickly in her life than she did on that day to return to her holiday hotel in the town. There she quickly found her brother Alfred, who was sitting in the lounge reading the Sunday newspapers as he waited for her to join him for lunch.

At first Alfred was somewhat sceptical about his sister's grim discovery, but she persuaded him that she was certain that it was a human arm she had seen and not a discarded mannequin's arm. Hastily he folded his newspapers, fetched his hat and accompanied his sister back to the bridge. Alfred, quite rightly, considered that he should first verify the find before bothering the police.

On arrival Alfred scrambled down the side of the ravine as his sister watched from the bridge. When he scrambled up again, his ashen complexion, white to the lips, told its own story. The pair then went to find a policeman. Because the area is sparsely populated, they had to call at Moffat police station to do so. There a car was made available to take Alfred back to the Gardenholme Linn; Susan was, understandably, disinclined to go with him and, after her eight-mile walk, she preferred to stay at the police station, fortified with a cup of coffee, to make a statement before returning to the hotel to wait for her brother. Neither of them was very keen on the idea of going into the dining-room for lunch now . . .

At the bridge, Alfred sat in the car while Sergeant Robert Sloan of the Dumfriesshire Constabulary scrambled down into the ravine. On the bank he found four bundles containing human remains, dismembered, mutilated and badly decomposed. The bundles, wrapped in newspapers, part of a cotton sheet, a pillow-slip and a woman's blouse, contained two upper arms, two lower legs, the upper portion of a female torso, two arm bones, two thigh bones, two lower leg bones, and a total of thirty pieces of flesh.

Later that afternoon a police transporter was sent out to the area to remove the remains and take them to Moffat police station for a preliminary examination by Professor John Glaister, Regius Professor of Forensic Medicine at Glasgow University, and Dr Gilbert Millar, Lecturer in Pathology at the University of Edinburgh. The following day a further search was made by a team of officers, who discovered a number of other items, including a left fore-arm and hand, a right forearm and hand, a left thigh, a pelvis and numerous scattered pieces of flesh. All these grim relics were wrapped in pieces of cotton sheeting and portions of various newspapers, including the *Sunday Graphic* dated 15 September 1935, the *Daily Herald* and the *Sunday Chronicle*.

After these further finds had been examined by the two

pathologists, they, together with the previous discoveries, were removed to the Department of Anatomy at Edinburgh University for further detailed study. Meanwhile a look-out was kept for other body parts which would make up the missing pieces of this human jigsaw puzzle. Vigilance paid off, and on 28 October a left foot, wrapped in part of a copy of the *Daily Herald* dated 31 August, was found, while on 4 November the final find was made: a right forearm and hand wrapped in a piece of a copy of the *Daily Herald* dated 2 September, and two gruesomely mutilated heads, bundled into a child's pair of woollen rompers. Further pieces of flesh were also found, contained in pages of the *Daily Herald* dated 5, 6 and 7 August respectively. Someone obviously stockpiled old newspapers . . .

The police had little to go on. They concluded that the remains had been dumped, most likely from a car, some time prior to 19 September when heavy rainstorms had raised the river levels, and that when the waters receded the parcels had been left high and dry on the bank. But nowhere in the area had anyone been reported missing, and no one had seen anyone acting suspiciously in the vicinity of the bridge.

Forensic examination of the remains was a most unpleasant task even for the pathologists who were used to work of this kind. The remains were in an advanced state of putrefaction consequent upon their long exposure to the open air, and were seething with maggots. They comprised a total of 70 separate pieces, and the finding of two heads, three female breasts, various duplications of limb bones, two portions of external female sexual organs and a womb, made it clear that two female bodies were involved. Several portions of the puzzle were missing, however, and these pieces were never found.

It was also clear to the pathologists that the person or persons who had dismembered the victims had a good knowledge of anatomy, since the limbs had been cleanly disarticulated at the joints – no amateurish sawing or hacking here. It appeared that sharp-bladed surgical insturments had been used. Furthermore, both bodies had been entirely drained of blood – again, a feature pointing to a person with specialized knowledge, since the average lay-man would not know how to go about this task.

The killer had gone to great lengths to obliterate all possible features whereby the victims could be identified. As well as removing the tips from all the fingers and extracting all the teeth, the eyes, ears, noses and lips, and large portions of skin had been removed. The feet had been extensively mutilated, especially in the case of one of the victims who seemed to be the older of the two; it was assumed that she had some foot deformity such as a bunion or enlarged joint which could have helped to identify her. This subsequently proved to be the case. Flesh had also been carved from legs, arms and torso to mask the fact that the older victim was much more heavily built than the younger woman.

While the pathologists were struggling to recreate the two bodies as completely as they could from this unpromising material, the police had their own problems. As we have seen, no one was missing in that part of Scotland, or even wider afield north of the Border; and not a single witness had come forward to report sighting anyone behaving in an odd or suspicious manner, either with or without a car, on or near the bridge over the Gardenholme Linn by day or by night in the latter half of September.

The police realized that it would be a well-nigh impossible task to try to identify the victims from incomplete bodies devoid of fingerprints, teeth or distinguishing physical characteristics. Instead, they turned their attention to the wrappings in which the remains had been found, and it was these that provided the breakthrough that they so sorely needed.

The rain-sodden pages of the *Sunday Graphic* dated 15 September were recognized as having formed part of what is known as a 'slip edition' – a special edition circulating in one particular district only – in this case the Lancaster and Morecambe area of Lancashire. The piece of paper bore the serial number 1067 and part of a photograph of two young girls, one with a crown, with a partly obliterated headline reading . . . AMBE'S CARNIVAL QUEEN CROWNED. It was one of 3,700 copies of a limited edition containing a news item about Morecambe's carnival queen having been crowned the previous day – a 'slip' edition. And it had been a fatal 'slip' on the murderer's part to use this paper to wrap the two women's remains, for it focused the attention of the police on his home district instead of Scotland and was to lead to his arrest.

Curiously, one of those rare coincidences occurred which no writer of detective fiction would dare use – it could happen only in real life! A few hours after the Chief Constable of Dumfriesshire had communicated his discovery to the Lancashire police, one of his officers drew his attention to a news item in the Glasgow-based *Daily Record* about the disappearance, three weeks earlier, of a young children's nursemaid from the house of a doctor in Lancaster, where she was employed to look after his three young children. The Chief Constable followed up this lead for what it was worth, and found that it was worth a great deal. The maid, Mary Jane Rogerson, it transpired, was not the only person to have disappeared from the doctor's household – his wife Isabella had also vanished at the same time. Two women missing – one young, one older. Three weeks ago – that would put the disappearance within the time frame pinpointed by the dates on the newspapers found in the ravine – one of which was the Lancaster 'slip' edition.

The Dumfriesshire police got in touch with the stepmother of the missing nursemaid. Since it was, of course, quite impossible to obtain an identification of the body, they arranged for her to be shown the woman's blouse and the child's rompers which had been found on the bank of the Gardenholme Linn. Mrs Rogerson recognized the two items immediately. The blouse had belonged to her stepdaughter, its identity made certain by a patch under one armpit, which Mrs Rogerson had sewn herself. She also recognized the rompers as a pair which she had seen the doctor's youngest child wearing, adding that her stepdaughter had been given some outgrown children's clothing by a woman friend and had passed them on to her employer's wife for the children. To clinch the matter, Mrs Rogerson identified a special knot in the elastic of the rompers which she had tied when she had had occasion to mend them.

The Lancaster Borough police now took over the investigation, acting on information given to them by the Dumfriesshire force. It was decided to make a start by interviewing the doctor who had employed the missing nursemaid. He had apparently called at the police station in Lancaster some two weeks or so previously, asking for help in locating his wife, who had left him. He stated that she had taken the nursemaid with her and that he was having to co-opt various neighbours to look after his children while he attended to his practice.

Dr Buck Ruxton was a native of Bombay. He had changed his name by deed poll from Bukhtyar Rustomji Ratanji Hakim, considering, no doubt, that his original name would be too much of a mouthful for his English panel patients. (The 'Hakim' part of his name was more or less a title, as it means 'Doctor'.) He obtained his Bachelor of Medicine and Bachelor of Surgery degrees at the University of Bombay, and after serving in the Indian Medical Service he came to London, where he took his postgraduate degrees at the city's university. He then took up a substantial practice in 1930 at 2 Dalton Square, Lancaster. He was thirty-one at that time.

Mrs Isabella Ruxton was the common-law wife of the doctor and was two years his junior. It was common knowledge that the couple were frequently engaged in wild and violent quarrels, mainly owing to the doctor's unfounded jealousy and highly strung, excitable nature. One moment they would be passionately devoted, the next the doctor would indulge in one of his wild outbursts of temper, screaming threats and abuse to his wife and occasionally using violence towards her. On two occasions in previous years the police had been summoned to the house, and several previously employed maids had left owing to the stress caused by the doctor's threats, including brandishing a knife, and the constant noise and rows.

When he called at the police station to report his wife and maid missing, on 4 October, he had behaved in an agitated way, babbling incoherently and even bursting into tears.

He alleged that a young solicitor, Robert Edmondson, who was employed in the Lancaster Corporation Town Clerk's Department, was her 'fancy man' and had incited her to run away with him. If that were the case, the police said, why would she take the maid with her?

The doctor bolstered up his story of the 'elopement' by telling the police how on a previous occasion Mrs Ruxton had gone to Edinburgh with the Edmondson family, with whom she was friendly, for a weekend trip. In Edinburgh Mrs Ruxton was to meet her sister, Mrs Nelson, and the party was to stay at the Adelphi Hotel, which they did. All the members of the party occupied separate rooms, and the young man had travelled in his parents' car with them, while Mrs Ruxton had travelled with the daughter of the family in her own car. But this outing, the doctor insisted, was just a cover-up for an illicit association between his wife and young Robert Edmondson, and he had left his practice unattended and followed them to the Edinburgh hotel in his own car, where he had made a scene. The police did not, of course, believe one word of these absurd allegations. They knew Edmondson and his impeccable reputation, and they also knew that the doctor was an unbalanced personality obsessed with an unreasonable jealousy. His wife's most innocent actions became completely distorted in his mind, to the point that he became paranoid about almost everything she did. They sent him home telling him that they would 'look into it'.

Ruxton was quickly back at the police station, soon after the reports of the finding of the bodies at Moffat had surfaced in the newspapers. He demanded to see the Chief Constable. 'There are a lot of rumours going around', Buxton complained, 'that those bodies at Moffat are our two. This publicity is ruining my practice! Can you not publish it in the papers that there is no connection between those bodies and our two? That would stop all this trouble.' The wildly excited doctor became totally incoherent and wept copiously as the Chief Constable assured him that as soon as he had satisfied himself that there was no connection between them, he would be happy to do so. This appeared to placate the doctor, who then went home.

Buck Ruxton's next call at the police station was at the request of the Chief Constable. He came quickly enough, and asked whether they had found his wife and the maid, and whether Edmondson was with them. Instead, the Chief Constable asked him to account for his own movements between 14 and 30 September. Ruxton made a long and involved statement, made some amendments and signed it, and then asked if he could go. He was persuaded to stay and during the remainder of the day he found himself being interviewed at length by a number of Scotland Yard officers. Eventually he was arrested and charged with the murder of Mary Rogerson, to which he replied, 'Most emphatically not! Of course not! The furthest thing from my mind. What motive and why? What are you talking?'

The following day Ruxton appeared in the local court, and was remanded in custody from week to week in that court until 5 November, when he was further charged with the murder of Isabella Ruxton. More evidence was brought on various dates, and on 13 December he was committed for trial at Manchester Assizes. He was committed on both charges, but in the event he was tried for the murder of Mrs Ruxton only, since the police had much more evidence of her murder than that of the maid.

After Ruxton's arrest the police made a detailed investigation of the house at 2 Dalton Square, and took away a number of articles for forensic examination. Among these was a sheet found on the bed in the room which was used as a bedroom by the doctor and his wife. This was the only sheet found on the bed, and it proved to have a vital part to play in the case. It was sent to Mr Barwick, an expert on textiles from the Manchester Chamber of Commerce Test Department, together with the portions of cotton sheet found at Moffat. Mr Barwick found them all to be identical in every respect and, in particular, that a specific fault in the selvedge was common to both the entire sheet taken from the bed and to the pieces of sheeting found with the remains. He said that the consistent presence of such a fault implied not only that the two sheets must have been a pair, but that they were the product of the same loom in manufacture, and that moreover they were the product of the same warp while on the loom. He added that this would not be found in all the output of that loom, but that it was a temporary defect which would rectify itself the next time a warp was put into the loom.

Asked later to specify in more detail, Mr Barwick stated that whereas the manufacturer's normal selvedge had twenty-six threads working in thirteen pairs, on this particular example three threads were missing, leaving twenty-two working in pairs plus one odd one. The same 23-thread selvedge was found in both the entire sheet and the torn pieces. Thus three missing threads took their places in the web of evidence which was slowly but surely enmeshing the prisoner.

While the police, together with forensic and other experts, were laboriously piecing together the basic facts which would make up the framework of their case, Buck Ruxton was in custody strenuously denying his guilt, although he did not attempt to deny that their relationship had been a stormy one, their life together a succession of high peaks of excitement alternating with deep troughs of despair. He even admitted that he was a jealous man, and continued to make references to Edmondson, the young solicitor. The young man's father, despite a friendship with the doctor's family going back some years, was beginning to weary of the Indian's scurrilous accusations against his son, and dismissed his claims as 'the ravings of an obsessional lunatic'. But murder? No way. His wife and his maid were more use to him alive than dead. Who would look after their three children? Who would cook, clean, wash and keep the house tidy? He had his surgery to keep him busy.

'You can tell all that to the judge,' the police told him.

The trial of Buck Ruxton opened on 2 March 1936 before Mr Justice Singleton at Manchester Assizes. Mr J. C. Jackson, KC, Mr Maxwell Fyfe, KC and Mr Hartley Shawcross were briefed for the Crown; Buck Ruxton was defended by Mr Norman Birkett, KC, supported by Mr Philip Kershaw, KC. Two of these men were to become future chancellors, and another, a most eminent judge. The trial was to last eleven days. While the prosecution presented no fewer than 106 witnesses, none was produced on the defendant's behalf. Ruxton alone was the witness for the defence, but his two days in the witness-box failed to disconcert him one whit, and for every question he had a glib and plausible answer.

The number of medical experts testifying at the trial was impressive, beginning with the aforementioned Professor Glaister and Dr Millar; Professor James C. Brash, Professor of Anatomy at the Edinburgh University; Dr Arthur C. W. Hutchinson, Dean of the Edinburgh Dental Hospital; and finally the famous Professor (later Sir) Sydney Smith, Regius Professor of Forensic Medicine of Edinburgh University. The evidence given by these eminent men took two days, and from this several pertinent facts emerged which left the prisoner's guilt in no doubt.

Firstly, the dismemberment and mutilation of the bodies had been carried out with the most exact precision by a person with not only sound anatomical knowledge but also with the instruments necessary to perform them. In addition, the bodies had been drained entirely of blood, a procedure possible only within hours of death and by a person with the surgical knowledge of how to effect it. A third very telling point was that the mutilations had been performed with the express purpose of concealing not only obvious points of identification such as fingerprints, but also less obvious ones, such as the fact that the older victim had a bunion or deformed bone in one great toe, a prominent nose, vaccination scars on one arm, and so on – even to the extent of removing skin and layers of fatty tissue from the body of one victim in an effort to obscure the fact that she was much more heavily built than her companion in death. This would, of course, imply that both victims were known to their murderer. Unfortunately for the killer, he had overlooked the fact that such precise surgical procedures as he had used would only serve to emphasize the obvious conclusion that a surgeon had performed them and thus draw attention to himself – he was a qualified surgeon. Thus his actions defeated their own object . . .

Further evidence showed that the hyoid bone in the neck

had been fractured in one of the bodies, the experts pointing out that this bone is rarely broken except by strangulation. They concluded, therefore, that the victim had been killed by asphyxiation, most likely by smothering with a pillow or some such object. The removal of the eyes from this body tended to corroborate this conclusion, since in such a case *petechiae* (small pin-point haemorrhages in the whites of the eyes) are an infallible sign. Very few people apart from medical men would have known this, and it is unlikely that a victim's eyes would have been removed merely on account of their colour, since this is no guide to identification. Thousands, probably millions, of people have eyes the same colour.

No two people, even twins, have identical fingerprints, however, but what is not generally known is that merely removing the *epidermis* (outer skin) does not remove the fingerprint pattern, and only the complete severing of the fingertips can effect this. Again, such removal in the case of these two bodies pointed to the knowledge of a medical man.

No sign of pregnancy was found in the womb of the younger victim, which effectively put paid to one of Buck Ruxton's later stories that his wife had taken the maid to Edinburgh to obtain an abortion – a story which he quickly concocted as soon as he realized that his tale of his wife's 'elopement to Edinburgh with Edmondson' was recognized for what it was – a complete fabrication.

Bloodstains found in the house were the next point to come under close scrutiny. A large quantity of bloodstains having been found on the stairs, Ruxton quickly trotted out another of his cooked-up excuses, this time that his wife had fallen on the stairs causing a miscarriage, and that she had bled copiously. It was quite true that Isabella Ruxton had suffered a miscarriage, but the doctor was found who had been called in by Ruxton to attend her, and he testified that this had occurred *three years previously*, in 1932! He also testified that Mrs Ruxton had told him that the miscarriage had occurred spontaneously (this is known in medical terms as an 'inevitable abortion') and that she had not had a fall, and that although she had bled profusely the bleeding was confined to her bed and had been mostly sopped up with towels. He was also able to remember quite clearly that there was no blood on the stairs.

Ruxton now had to think quickly and devise a fiction to account for *fresh* bloodstains on the stairs. He said that shortly after his wife and the maid had left him with no one to look after the children, he had cut his hand very badly when opening a can of fruit for the children's breakfast. Under cross-examination, he admitted that a can of peaches was, perhaps, rather an unusual item on the breakfast table, but he pointed out that with no women in the house to prepare the children's meals he was obliged to use whatever was at hand. The older children confirmed that they had never at any time been given canned peaches for breakfast, to which Ruxton replied that after cutting himself when trying to open the can he had thrown it in the dustbin unopened, together with the tin-opener he had used. However, no such can, either unopened or otherwise, nor a tin-opener, had been found in or about the house. Asked why he had, purportedly, thrown away a full can of fruit, he said that he was in a bad temper from having cut his hand so badly and just wanted to get rid of the thing that had caused it. As to the tin-opener, the same applied to that also. Asked why he would destroy such a useful object, he said that it was not useful if it did not work properly.

His hand had certainly been cut very severely, even though the prosecution was convinced that this had occurred, not by a tin-opener, but by the slip of a scalpel while dismembering the bodies. There was a diagonal gash across three fingers, exposing the bone in one of them. Ruxton decided against seeing a doctor about it but instead went to a neighbour, who dressed his hand for him. Her husband, present at the time, observed that 'it must be a funny kind of tin-opener to cause wounds like that'. This is probably why Ruxton did not show his hand to another doctor – who would almost certainly query how he had come by such an injury. It was a certainty that such a wound would bleed profusely, and this Ruxton used as his excuse for blood on the stairs and also on his clothing and other items in the house.

However badly a hand were cut in this manner, it would certainly not account for the quantities of blood which were proved to have been shed on the stairs. Buck Ruxton had taken up the stair-carpet and given it to his cleaning lady and cook. The cleaning lady said she did not want it, so the cook opted to take the carpet, first attempting to clean it in the backyard of the doctor's house.

In her evidence the cook, Mrs Elizabeth Curwen, stated that she had attempted to clean the carpets with a yard brush and several buckets of water, but she could not get rid of the stains, and so abandoned the attempt and decided to leave them. Subsequently, Ruxton offered the carpet, along with some other items, to a patient, Mrs Mary Hampshire, who was also a family friend and neighbour. This lady also attempted to clean the carpet, using the same method.

'I laid the carpet in the backyard,' she testified at the trial, 'and threw about twenty or thirty buckets of water on it to try to wash the blood off, and the colour of the water that came off was like blood. I threw it on the line and left it to dry, and when it was washday I had another go at it with the yard brush and water and still could not get the congealed blood off.' It seems probable that, like Mrs Curwen, she abandoned the attempt and left it.

Another of the items that Ruxton had given to Mrs Hampshire was a blue suit of good quality, badly stained with blood, which the doctor told her had come from his injured hand. She had told him that she would have it cleaned. The following morning the doctor called at the Hampshires' house at about nine o'clock, looking, as that lady was later to describe, very ill. In contrast to his usually smart appearance, he was unshaven, wore no collar and tie, had his hand heavily bandaged, and was wearing a shabby old raincoat. Mrs Hampshire commented to him on his unwell appearance, to which he replied that 'he had not slept a wink all night' owing to the throbbing pain in his injured hand. He told her that he had come to ascertain what articles she and her husband had removed from his house. She told him that they had taken three carpets from the waiting-room and the blue suit.

As soon as she mentioned the suit, Ruxton seemed, she later said, to become agitated. He asked to see it. Mrs Hampshire took it from a table in the kitchen and handed it to him. He said that he would take it to be cleaned, but she told him not to bother. 'I told him that, since he had been good enough to give us the suit, I could surely pay for the cleaning,' she said.

Ruxton then pointed out the tailor's tab and another tab bearing his (Ruxton's) name. He asked Mrs Hampshire to cut them out and destroy them. She said she would do this later, but he insisted that it be done immediately. He asked for a pair of scissors but found that, owing to the injury to his right hand, he could not cut out the tabs, and Mrs Hampshire did this for him. He then told her to burn them, and she threw them on the fire. She considered his actions very odd, to say the least.

Returning home after visiting Mrs Hampshire, Ruxton found Mrs Oxley, the cleaning lady, waiting for him on the doorstep, unable to gain admittance. She noted the doctor's unaccustomed dishevelled appearance, and he told her of the pain from his injured hand having kept him awake all night. She made him some coffee and changed the dressing and bandages on his hand, noting that it bled afresh as soon as the previous pad was removed. She said that the doctor should send for his wife to come back from her trip if he was so ill.

Ruxton then burst into tears and slumped with his head in his hands. 'I lied to you,' he told Mrs Oxley. 'My wife has not gone on a trip. She has run off with another man. I am the most unhappy man in the world! She has left me with the three children. You make a friend of a man,' he continued amid sobs, 'you treat him as a friend and he eats at your table, and he makes love to your wife behind your back. It is terrible! I could forgive extravagance or anything else, but never infidelity! My God – what did I do to deserve this? A solicitor too – he should know better!'

Soon, however, the doctor recovered himself, realizing that he had patients waiting. Mrs Oxley helped him into the surgery and quickly tidied it while he took a spare collar and tie from a drawer and put them on, having thrown the old raincoat into a closet. Mrs Oxley then made him another cup of coffee and saw him take two white tablets, which he told her were 'to steady his nerves'. He then opened his surgery.

Dustmen who that same day came to empty the refuse bins testified that they noted a number of heavily blood-stained articles in the dustbins and lying around in the backyard, including towels, a partly burned shirt, carpets and rugs, and a blue dress, also partly burned, with glass buttons. There was also a heap of what looked like plaster and wallpaper scraped from a wall lying on the ground. This material had a number of what looked like bloodstains on it. One of the men asked Ruxton whether he had had an accident, and the doctor spun him the tale of the tin-opener's cutting his hand and almost severing a finger. Not seeing Mrs Ruxton around as the man usually did on these occasions, he asked the doctor if she was away; to this inquirer he said that she was 'touring in her car'.

The following morning Mrs Oxley came as usual, and this time Ruxton told her to clean upstairs. Recalled to the witness-box, she described how she found the bath to be stained a dirty yellow colour to within six inches from the top, and despite strenuous scrubbing with Vim, she could not get it clean. She also noticed some blood on the wall above the bath, about three feet from the floor. Under cross-examination, Ruxton strenuously denied that the stains were blood, averring that they were rust stains from the geyser!

'What – on the whole of the interior of the bath, and even on the wall above? If anyone would believe that, they would believe anything!' the prosecutor exclaimed.

Replying to questions about his reactions to complaints by his servants about a noisome smell in the house, against which he was observed to spray eau-de-Cologne, he insisted that this was caused by old wallpaper paste and size when the wall above the staircase was stripped.

Buck Ruxton had no glib excuse, however, when asked point-blank whether he had killed his wife; he just denied all knowledge of her death to the very end. It was considered by most persons present at the trial that they had quarrelled after Mrs Ruxton had returned home from a car trip late at night, probably to see her sister, and he had accused her of having been out with Edmondson. In his fury he had killed her, and on hearing her screams the maid had rushed out of her room to the landing where they were struggling. When he realized that his wife was dead, he seized the maid and cut her throat, knowing that she had seen him commit murder and could and most likely would go to the police and eventually testify against him. Many such double murders are committed because the killer has to silence the witness to his crime.

This trial was a sensational one from start to finish, but the greatest sensation was the Cyclops eye. In the words of Thomas De Quincey: 'But what was Cyclops doing here?'

The discovery of a Cyclops eye among the remains found in the ravine at Moffatt was the most unusual feature of the case, and although a number of witnesses, mainly medical men, were cross-examined about it, no definite conclusion was reached as to its connection with the case. Indeed, Mr Justice Singleton, in his summing-up, appeared to give the impression that he did not attach much significance to it.

The condition known in medical terms as 'cyclopia' is an extremely rare malformation, in which the two eyes have become more or less fused together during foetal development and appear as a single eye in the middle of the forehead. Though of extreme rarity in man, it occurs slightly more frequently in the pig. It is accompanied by other defects in development and the individual does not survive more than a few hours at most.

The name of the condition is of course derived from Greek myth: a race of one-eyed giants who forged thunderbolts for the god Zeus.

A number of tests were made on the Cyclops eye found with the remains at Moffat, and Professor Brash, after a critical examination, gave his considered opinion that the eye was that of a pig and not human, and also that it appeared to have been preserved, probably in spirit or formalin, so that it presented all the appearances of a museum or laboratory specimen. This probability was corroborated because the optic nerve had been cut cleanly across in a manner which could not have occurred if the eye had been left as a residue from other tissues which had decomposed, or had been consumed by rats or other vermin.

A fanciful theory was put forward, based on statements Ruxton had made to neighbours, that Mary Rogerson had been pregnant and had been taken to Edinburgh by his wife in order to procure an abortion. This, it seems, had been merely a 'cover-up story' to explain the absence of his wife and the maid to close friends, who were also neighbours. He never at any time advanced this theory to the court during his trial, but maintained that he had no knowledge of either their whereabouts or their deaths. According to the 'pregnancy' theory, the maid had given birth to a child afflicted with cyclopia. This, Professor Brash stated unequivocally, was patently ridiculous.

First of all, the maid was never pregnant. This was proved by the condition of the younger victim's womb which was consistent with that of a virgin. Secondly, recently used sanitary pads were found in her room after her disappearance. Thirdly, the cyclops eye was in a condition consistent with having been taken from a full-term foetus; such a condition could not have arisen in a foetus from an early abortion. Fourthly, Professor Brash would stake his reputation that the cyclops eye was from a pig anyway!

Buck Ruxton was known to be interested in ophthalmology, and this would, of course, include abnormal conditions of the eye, both human and animal. A much more likely theory, to my mind, is that he had possessed such a specimen, and that this was preserved in formalin or alcohol. He may have needed spirit or formalin while dismembering the bodies of his victims and, afraid to draw attention to himself by purchasing a quantity of either of these substances, of which he was perhaps in short supply at the time, he poured the contents of the specimen jar into the vessel he was using, inadvertently pouring out the eye with it. In his haste and confusion, he had not noticed this. Alternatively, he may have deliberately included the eye among the remains he deposited at Moffat, hoping thereby to cloud the issue.

The issue was not clouded when the jury retired to consider their verdict. On 13 March 1936, the eleventh day of the trial, they were out for only one hour and four minutes before returning a unanimous verdict of guilty. Buck Ruxton was sentenced to death, and the Court of Criminal Appeal dismissed his application for appeal against the sentence on 27 April. On 12 May he was hanged at Strangeways Prison, Manchester. Though the question of his sanity was never at issue – at least in the medico-legal sense – he was insane enough in the popular use of the word, to imagine that he could commit two such ghastly murders and get away with his crime.

An interesting point arises from this trial. I cannot do better than quote Mr Justice Singleton's words on the matter, which proves him to be a most humane judge, even allowing that he had no choice in hanging this grisly parody of a doctor. His exemption of the all-male jury from further jury service would appear to be unique in the annals of British criminal history:

> Members of the jury, I desire to say how much I appreciate the care and attention which you have given to this case. It has been a very heavy duty which has been cast upon you . . . You have been faced with the most dreadful and gruesome details such as few jurors have had to encounter, and I think it is only right that I should recommend that you are not again called upon as jurors . . . Will you . . . make sure, before you leave these premises, that your names are entered?

7

Passion at the Villa Madeira

Alma Rattenbury and George Stoner
(1935)

The concept of the so-called 'toy boy' is not new. The pages of history are replete with examples of older women taking youths as lovers, from the days of Ancient Greece right through the centuries. Neither does Hollywood have a monopoly in our own time, despite the much publicized affairs of some stars with young men in some cases younger than their own sons. But in very few, if any, of these passionate liaisons does the inevitable jealousy have the effect of sending the youthful admirer after the beloved's husband with a mallet to hit him over the head – which is what George Stoner did in 1935 in Bournemouth.

Francis Rattenbury, a distinguished architect, was fifty-seven when he married his second wife, Alma, who was twenty-five years his junior. For her it was also a second marriage; by her first marriage she had had a son, Christopher, who attended boarding-school near Christchurch, and came home for the holidays. The Rattenburys had a son, John, in 1929. From all accounts the couple were very happy. He told his sister: 'I have a wonderfully happy home – bright, joyous and full of fun all the time', and went on to say that his wife was a very lovable person and that he could not imagine life without her. Everyone, he said, loved her – men, women and children – even animals.

When Francis Rattenbury was sixty-three he purchased a house in Manor Road, Bournemouth, named Villa Madeira, and he became semi-retired, taking the odd private commission from time to time, and investing in gilt-edged securities and real property. Alma was a talented musician, who in her younger days had composed songs for a living. Now she looked after her wealthy husband with what he described as fondness and devotion, though she was not a little perturbed by the increasingly large quantities of whisky he had by now made a habit of imbibing every evening. John, too – now six years old – needed love and attention, together with his older half-brother when he was home for the holidays. She therefore had plenty to do, and still found time for entertaining her husband's business associates, tending the garden, and her music.

The Rattenburys employed but one maid, Irene Riggs, who preferred to be called a household help. She and Alma soon became close friends after she had joined the family. Alma was never one to be snobbish and often said she cared not one jot about social class. Some of her friends, who secretly envied her fine clothes, Daimler car and glamorous lifestyle, often wondered . . . Her husband allowed her a thousand pounds a year – quite a tidy sum in 1934 – and she also received royalties from music publishers for her songs: her output was still quite prolific.

At about this time Rattenbury no longer wanted to drive his car himself, and advertised for a 'willing lad, able to drive' to act as handyman-cum-chauffeur. The choice they made was George Stoner, who was actually only nineteen but gave his age as twenty-two. His duties were to drive the car, take John to school and collect him in the afternoons, and to do a few jobs around the house and garden. The son of a bricklayer, Stoner was a pleasant enough chap, reasonably good-looking, and with a friendly and open manner. He was hired at one pound per week but, it seems, he had quite a few perks such as being told to keep the change when sent to the shops with five pounds by Alma for items that were needed in the household.

Rattenbury, though still on affectionate terms with his wife and nicknamed 'Rats' by her, was becoming more and more withdrawn and depressed, almost reclusive. A disastrous business deal in property had caused him much misgiving: it made his financial position rather more precarious than he would have liked. By sinking a half-bottle of whisky, however, he could contrive not to think about it.

Not surprisingly, he began to neglect his marital duties, and in fact began to lose interest in Alma altogether, even in her music, of which he had previously been a great devotee. Naturally, Alma did not fail to notice the profound change in her husband, although she did make an effort to keep things on an even keel and continue to show him wifely devotion.

However, the void in Alma's life soon yearned for fulfilment, and she then sought the companionship of the young chauffeur more and more. Even her close friendship with Irene Riggs was jeopardized, that lady complaining that her mistress was beginning to prefer Stoner's company to hers. As to Francis Rattenbury, it was doubtful that he even noticed; he spent most of his time in a whisky-induced stupor.

Stoner's bedroom was just across the landing from Alma's (by this time she no longer shared a bedroom with her husband) and thus it was easy for the two to visit each other's rooms. It is not certain when the two became lovers – probably in November 1934, when Alma made a pretext of a non-existent medical condition to visit London 'to see a specialist'. Instead, Alma and her chauffeur stayed at a hotel. Later Alma concocted a story about requiring a minor operation, saying she would go into a private nursing home rather than a hospital in London. Again Alma and her lover went off to the capital, this time for three days.

By now Alma was undoubtedly deeply in love with Stoner, and the words of her latest songs expressed the reawakening of her youth which her affair with a boy of nineteen had brought her. He no longer kept up the fiction that he was twenty-two. Alma, now thirty-eight, sincerely loved her 'toy boy', but since his conquest of her he had changed from an unassuming, even quietly spoken, young man to a brash, self-assertive and domineering individual. Heedless of his position in the household as an employee, he even went so far as to tell her what to do. He told her to give up drinking cocktails before dinner; she did his bidding. He told her he disliked her dressing in certain colours, and she gave the offending clothes to Irene Riggs who, overjoyed at receiving dresses in *haute-couture* materials not normally affected by a housemaid, was not one to question why. Alma seemed to enjoy a certain degree of domination by Stoner, but at one point she tried to end their affair after a particularly vociferous quarrel. Stoner would not even entertain the idea; who, he reasoned, would be so foolish as to give up a rich and beautiful woman who took him to London in her Daimler and stayed in the best hotels, and who took him to Harrods on these occasions, buying him silk shirts and pyjamas, gold cufflinks and tie-pins, and top-quality Havanna cigars? It was almost too good to be true. They made it up.

The truth that Stoner did not know was that it was too good to last. From a humble background he had suddenly been catapulted into a world of high-society affluent life-styles, which was far removed from anything he was used to, and it had gone to his head. He was now arrogant and overbearing. And always, festering on the inside, like a maggot in the heart of an outwardly sound apple, Stoner's jealousy of Alma's husband would raise its ugly head.

On the evening of 22 March 1935 Alma and Stoner returned from their three-day London trip. Francis Ratten-bury was already in bed. It was about 10.30 when Alma went up to his room to bid him goodnight. He had drunk a good deal of whisky and was in a thoroughly inebriated mood. He did not even ask her how the 'operation' she was supposed to have undergone had progressed, though he did note that she was in a good humour.

The next morning Rattenbury was in one of his periodic bouts of depression – backed up, no doubt, by a massive hangover. Alma decided that an outing would cheer him up and that some fresh air would do him good, so she made him a strong black coffee – he could not face food – and took him out in the car – Stoner, of course, at the wheel – to the Treetop Kennels a few miles out into the surrounding countryside, to see her dog which had been boarded there when about to produce a litter. The puppies had now been born, and the family spent a pleasant morning admiring them and fussing over their pedigree bitch.

The rest of that Sunday passed uneventfully enough. It

was Irene Riggs's Sunday off, so Alma cooked the traditional Sunday dinner herself, after which she played with
John and read to him while her husband went upstairs for a
snooze, as was his custom. Since Irene was out, it was
Stoner's turn to prepare tea, which he did at their customary hour of 4.30. Rattenbury was still in a rather depressed
mood, and Alma thought to herself that he needed something more than a short outing to see the dogs to dismiss it.
She suggested a day trip the next day to London, but her
husband pooh-poohed the idea. She then thought of a trip
to see his friend Mr Jenks, who lived in Bridport. Rattenbury liked this idea better and told his wife to telephone Mr
Jenks after tea to arrange something.

Mr Jenks was delighted at the suggestion, and said that
they should stay at his house on the Monday night so as to
avoid the long drive back to Bournemouth the same day. It
was at this point in the conversation that Stoner entered the
room and overheard Alma agreeing to Mr Jenks's suggestion that she and her husband stay the night at his house.

'You will not go to Bridport!' Stoner stormed as Alma
replaced the receiver. 'Over my dead body! And if you do
go, I will not drive you!'

'In Heaven's name, what's the matter with you?' Alma
said as her lover advanced towards her with flushed face
and voice thick with suppressed anger.

'I know what you will do! You will share a bedroom with
Rats while you are there – I know!'

'What rubbish!' Alma countered. 'Mr Jenks has a much
bigger house than ours – we can have separate rooms.'

'That may be – but you'd never dare ask him to give you
separate rooms – and Rats wouldn't dare ask him, either.
Just think what it would look like!'

'Well, I shall go, whether you like it or not!' Alma
retorted.

'I'll drive Rats to Bridport while you stay here with John
and Irene,' Stoner said.

'That would look just as bad,' Alma said. 'No, if we go,
then we all go.'

'But not with me driving you!' With this parting rejoinder
he flung out of the room, muttering fiercely to himself.

Alma dismissed this outburst with a shrug, knowing her 'toy boy' to be highly strung and excitable these days – a thing he never was before their affair began. She put it all down to the impetuosity of youth. He would grow out of it . . . She turned her attention to packing the things she and John, as well as her husband, would need for their overnight stay in Bridport on the morrow. Irene asked if she could help, but Alma declined the offer. 'We shan't need a lot,' she explained. 'It's not as if we were going on a holiday.'

Later that evening she played several card games with her husband, while he consumed ever more glasses of whisky. At about ten o'clock he looked as though he was going to fall asleep in his armchair, and cards would fall out of his hand almost as soon as he picked them up, so Alma bade him good-night and told him that she would go up to bed so as to be able to make an early start on their trip the next morning.

Alma completed the packing of the overnight cases containing the things that she, her husband and John would need, then she went along to Irene Riggs's room for her usual chat before turning in. She said good-night to her friend, returned to her room and put on her pyjamas ready for bed.

She was about to climb into bed a few minutes later when Stoner rushed into her room, seemingly out of breath and agitated. She had not seen him at all during the evening and presumed that he had gone out for a walk to cool off after his temper tantrum of the earlier part of the evening. Although Stoner normally served them coffee and biscuits – or sometimes cocoa – before they retired for the night, Alma had done this in his absence, and her husband had not even noticed the difference.

'What on earth is the matter?' cried Alma in some alarm.

'I'm really in trouble now,' he replied.

'Well, what is it? You can tell me.'

'You will not be going to Bridport tomorrow. I have hurt Rats!'

Alma was at a loss to understand the import of his words. 'You have hurt Rats? How?'

'I hit him over the head.'

Alma jumped up from the bed and rushed downstairs, followed closely by Stoner. She heard her husband's voice – a subdued groan. She was horrified to find 'Rats' slumped in his armchair, blood streaming from his head. She rubbed his hands, but they were cold. She shook him by the shoulders. 'Can you say anything?' she cried. There was no response. 'My God, he's dead!' she screamed to Stoner. 'You've killed him! What did you do it with?'

'A mallet from the woodshed,' he replied, far more calmly than he probably felt.

'Where is it now?' she asked.

'I put it back in the shed,' he said.

Alma felt an unreal sense of being just an onlooker sweep over her. It was as though she were at the cinema, watching a film in which things were happening, but not to her. Then she looked at Stoner, and looked at her dead husband crumpled up in his armchair, and started screaming uncontrollably. She screamed for Irene, who hastily flung on a dressing-gown and rushed downstairs. Alma then grabbed the decanter and a large glass and poured herself a whisky, and was promptly sick.

Irene Riggs called a doctor, and wrapped a wet white towel around the dead man's head. A Dr O'Donnell soon arrived, pronounced Francis Rattenbury dead and called the police. Alma was told to dress and informed that she and Stoner were going to be taken to the police station pending inquiries into the death of Francis Rattenbury at the Villa Madeira.

*   *   *

The trial of Alma Rattenbury and George Stoner opened at the Old Bailey on 27 May 1935 before Mr Justice Humphreys. By 8 a.m. more than a hundred people were outside the court hoping for a place in the public gallery. The night preceding the trial saw a number of jobless men camping outside, the idea being to sell their places in the morning to would-be spectators. The police continually harried them with flashlights to awaken them and move them on. One of these men with an entrepreneurial turn of mind set up a makeshift stall and sold hot coffee and rolls, of which even the police were glad, so they raised little objection.

Mr R. P. Croom-Johnson prosecuted, Mr T. J. O'Connor defended Alma Rattenbury, while Stoner's counsel was Mr J. D. Casswell. Mr Casswell considered it inappropriate to hold a joint trial for both the accused; only bias and prejudice, he averred, could result from this almost middle-aged woman and her teenage lover being tried together. He made a most determined attempt to persuade Mr Justice Humphreys to agree to separate trials and to make an order accordingly, but this application was refused. 'I see no ground for directing that there should be separate trials in this case,' was his terse wording.

A jury of ten men and two women had been empanelled. Both the accused pleaded not guilty, and each tried valiantly to protect the other partner in crime. The mallet which Stoner had used to bludgeon his employer to death was produced in court, gasps of horror going up when the prosecutor pointed to bloodstains and hairs which still adhered to it.

The conflicting statements which Alma had made when apprehended caused quite a stir in the court. The first words she uttered to the doctor after finding her husband's body were alleged to have been, 'Look at him! Look at the blood! Someone has finished him off!' Later, she was alleged to have said, 'I know who did it.' After an officer had cautioned her, she was said to have replied, 'I did it with a mallet. It is hidden. Rats has lived too long. No, my lover did it.' At the time she made these contradictory statements, she was obviously drunk and hysterical. It is said that she even tried to kiss a policeman. The doctor, who was present at the time, gave her an injection of morphia as a sedative and told Irene Riggs to put her to bed, but she came downstairs again.

The prosecution's main objective was to prove that the murder had been planned – a conspiracy between Alma Rattenbury and Stoner to kill Francis Rattenbury, the husband who stood in their way. For Stoner, it was admitted in evidence that he had taken the car to fetch Dr O'Donnell on Irene Riggs's instructions 'so that the doctor could get there sooner', although, as we have seen, this was too late to save the stricken man. Much was made of the fact that Alma had drunk a large quantity of whisky, to which, unlike her late husband, she was not accustomed – hence her incomprehensible behaviour after the discovery of her husband's body.

Stoner sat through his trial impassive, hardly moving except occasionally to brush back from his face a strand of his fair hair which had fallen forward. He was neatly attired in a grey suit and dark tie. He seemed to take no interest in the witnesses or even in the woman who was being tried with him, but appeared to be concentrating intently on the judge and counsel as they asked questions. Only once did he show any signs of emotion, and that was when Alma Rattenbury was laying bare the intimate details of their consuming passion, ending with the words 'I loved him' in a barely audible voice.

The defence sought to prove that when the fatal blow was struck the intention had been not to murder but merely to disable and thus to prevent the proposed trip to Bridport which had caused such intense jealousy on Stoner's part. As to Alma's defence, O'Connor took pains to point out that she was on trial not for having committed adultery but for murder, and that there was no evidence whatsoever that she had committed such a crime, nor conspired with her lover to kill her husband. He asked the jury not to be prejudiced against her merely because she had broken two of the most deep-rooted taboos in British society's moral code: having sexual relations with a servant, and having them with a mere boy half her age. He emphasized the incongruity of this latter taboo, pointing out that if an older man had relations with a young girl half his age, no stigma would attach to him merely on this account – unless, of course, the girl were under age. He enjoined the jury to think only in terms of the charge of murder, and to confine their attention strictly to the matter of the indictment.

The jury retired at 2.48 p.m. on the fifth day of the trial, remaining out for fifty minutes. The court was tensely hushed as they filed back. They had acquitted Alma Rattenbury, but found George Stoner guilty of murder. As they pronounced their verdict, Alma took a step forward in the dock and threw out her arms in a gesture of despair. 'Oh, no!' she cried in a tortured voice, 'Oh, no!' She swayed in the dock and was supported by the prison matrons who had stood beside her, and as they took her down the steps from the dock, the boy Stoner was left standing alone, a lost soul in his own private hell.

*   *   *

Women wept openly in the public gallery. The two women of the jury averted their gaze from the accused as he stood, stunned, while the clerk handed the court record book to the judge and he entered the verdicts. Then the judge asked Stoner if he wished to say anything before sentence, as is the customary procedure. 'Nothing at all, sir,' he replied. Those were the only words he had spoken throughout his trial.

A recommendation of mercy had been made, and the judge informed Stoner, after sentencing him to death, that this recommendation would be relayed to the proper channels. Two warders took him below, and there he passed Alma Rattenbury on her way to freedom, her pale face smudged with weeping. She tried to speak to him, but no sound escaped her lips. Stoner's arms were held tightly to his sides by the two guards, and all he could do was smile weakly at the woman he had loved with such disastrous consequences. It was the last time they met.

Mrs Rattenbury was taken from the court by Irene Riggs in a cab to the home of her late husband's nephew, a solicitor, but to their dismay, a large, hostile crowd had followed them and gathered outside the house. The solicitor telephoned the police and had the street cleared, but the odd few reporters still managed to get through. Alma was in a state of collapse, and the solicitor called a doctor, a Harley Street specialist named Dr Bathurst, who immediately arranged for Alma to be admitted to a private nursing home.

On the following morning, the worst of the shock had

passed and she seemed considerably improved. Irene Riggs came to see her with a bouquet of roses, and they had a long chat. Their friendship had survived the ordeals they had both been through – Alma as a defendant, Irene a witness. Alma had a photograph of Stoner by her bedside, and could barely take her eyes from it.

At 10 p.m. on the night of 3 June someone informed the matron that Alma was packing her things ready to leave. 'One look at her,' the matron said, 'showed me that nothing I or anyone else could say would prevent her from going if she wanted to . . . As she was a private patient, I had no authority to keep her against her will.' So Alma drove off in a hired car with her friend, who took her to another nursing home, where there was less supervision and she could come and go at will. The following morning she went out and walked about the streets, returning at midday. She went out again at 3.30 p.m., saying she would be back in the evening. With two pounds she had borrowed from her friend, she went to Waterloo and took the train to Bournemouth, alighting at Christchurch. But she did not go to Christopher's boarding-school; instead, she walked by the River Avon, where she sat on the bank at a point known as Three Arches Bend. She lit a cigarette, then took pencil and paper from her handbag and wrote a note on an old envelope. 'One must be bold to do a thing like this,' the note concluded. 'It is beautiful here, and I am alone. Thank God for peace at last.'

The peace she sought was in the waters of the Avon, clothed with flag irises along the banks and water-lilies on the water surface. A passing farm labourer saw her from the opposite bank. He saw her take a knife from her handbag, stab herself in the chest and pitch forward into the water. He was too far away to save her, and anyway, as he said later, he could not swim. He ran for help, and her body was recovered and taken to the Public Assistance Institution at Fairmile House in Christchurch.

Acquitted, but self-condemned, was the *Sunday Dispatch* headline. The news of her suicide was conveyed to Stoner in the condemned cell in Pentonville. He broke down and wept.

Although her friends had done their best to keep the time and locale of Alma's funeral a secret, hundreds of people were milling in the cemetery in Wimborne Road, Bournemouth, on Saturday, 8 June as she was laid to rest. Police were rushed to the scene, eventually having to control a crowd of more than 3,000, many of them women, who were trampling over graves and climbing headstones in order to reach vantage-points. A short private service, to which only the chief mourners were admitted, was held in the cemetery chapel. The doors were locked to keep out the huge crowd which tried to enter, disturbing the service with their noise. Among the crowd a man was going from one person to another obtaining signatures to a petition for the reprieve of George Stoner.

After the funeral the police had more headaches as souvenir-hunters besieged the Villa Madeira and broke into the house, chipping bloodstained plaster and wallpaper from the walls, digging up plants from the garden and stealing various small items. Other trespassers picnicked in the garden. Finally notices were put up by the police stating that legal action would be taken against any further persons entering the property.

The campaign for Stoner's reprieve meanwhile gathered momentum. The main reasons put in his favour were his extreme youth and the assumption that he had fallen under the influence of a dominating older woman. His dignified demeanour at his trial was also cited. In the end, a total of more than 320,000 signatures was obtained, and Casswell backed up the success of this campaign by appealing to the Court of Criminal Appeal. Stoner's execution had been fixed for 18 June, but was now postponed pending the appeal. This was heard on 24 June by Lord Chief Justice Hewart, Mr Justice Swift and Mr Justice Lawrence. London was engulfed in a sweltering heatwave at the time, in which sandwich-board men paraded outside the court carrying placards proclaiming: STONER MUST BE REPRIEVED – STOP THE LAW KILLING THIS BOY – END CAPITAL PUNISHMENT.

Stoner's appeal was dismissed. The judges saw no reason to reverse their original decision. Stoner looked dazed by the decision, but did not speak.

On the following day the Home Secretary decided to reprieve Stoner, commuting the death sentence to one of penal servitude for life. The Home Secretary is not called to give his reasons in such cases.

If only Alma Rattenbury had delayed her suicide bid, she might never have made it, had she known that her lover would not die. Presumably, he would be paroled in time, and they could again find the happiness they had once shared. But it was not to be. Stoner served only seven years of his sentence, having been a model prisoner. On his release he joined the army, and took part in the Dunkirk evacuation, after which he seems to have faded into obscurity. Perhaps that was what he wanted.

8

Tinker, Taylor, Soldier . . .

Marcus Marymont (1958)

It is a popular misconception that a serving American soldier, airman or sailor cannot be tried in a British court of justice for a crime committed on British soil but must be tried in his own country. Not so – and it is perfectly logical to process the perpetrator of a crime on British soil through the British judicial system, whether he be British, American, or hail from Timbuktu. The case of US Master Sergeant Marcus Marymont, who murdered his wife in order to be free to marry another woman, is a case in point, which also claims the distinction of being the first case of an American serviceman to be tried in Britain on a capital charge.

Marymont, in his late thirties, was tall and good-looking, and after seeing service in Japan during the war and in various parts of his native United States, he was posted in 1956 to the US Air Force base at Sculthorpe, in Norfolk. Relations between the sergeant and his wife, Mary Helen, who was a few years his senior, were somewhat strained, and had been so for some considerable time before this posting. The Sculthorpe base was a large one and there was a good deal of social life among the American community, and Marymont threw himself into the gay whirl of parties, where he soon gained a reputation for being fun-loving and extrovert.

The social life on the base, however, was not enough for the outgoing Marymont, who lost no opportunity of visiting Bushey Park, near London, where the US Air Force had their headquarters and provided a large choice of seminars and courses for Air Force personnel. An easy run-out from London and its environs was to Maidenhead in Berkshire, where there was a nightclub popular with US servicemen. One night Marymont joined a party of friends visiting this spot, and while at the club he met a vivacious young woman, Cynthia Taylor, who was separated from her husband. Only twenty-two, she was already manageress of a large commercial enterprise. Marymont was quite frank with her and told her that he was a married man with three children, but he lied when he told her that his family was in the States. It was not long before they were engaged in a passionate affair, and although American service personnel are well paid by British service standards, Marymont soon found himself getting into debt, because his expenses on the base were high and he was not really in a position to afford the presents which he was giving regularly to Mrs Taylor. But he continued to give her them and to run up unpaid bills in the sergeants' mess.

Marymont was soon deeply in love with Cynthia Taylor, who had a three-month-old baby. The sergeant told her that as soon as he was free he would marry her, and urged her to obtain a divorce so that she too would be free. With their marriage, he said, he would adopt her child and bring it up as his own.

Meanwhile, back at Sculthorpe, the rumours were circulating and instead of the wife being the last to know, as is so often the case, she was one of the first. Marymont was incredibly careless in the way he conducted his affair: it was almost as if he wished his wife to find out. He left an unposted letter to Mrs Taylor lying about in full view; Mrs Marymont opened it and its contents left her in no doubt about her husband's relationship with the younger woman. She shrank from a confrontation, but wrote a note to her husband asking him to tell her whether he loved her or this girl, and if it was the girl, what he proposed to do about the matter. Marymont threw the note into the fire and brazened it out. 'Of course there is no one else,' he said. 'What nonsense! I go to a party at a club with friends and your rumour-mongering women friends cook up these silly stories because they have nothing better to do, and you are silly enough to believe them!' Mrs Marymont may have believed him – at least for a time – more because she wanted to believe him than from any feeling of conviction that he was telling the truth.

His running up debts in the mess brought Nemesis on his head in the form of warnings from his officers, who were aware of the reasons behind this sudden financial instability in a man who had hitherto always paid his way. He was told he could find himself in serious financial trouble, quite apart from the emotional involvement behind it, but, as usual, he managed to talk his way out of the situation. But now he had to think of some way of solving his problems . . .

In the spring of 1958 Mary Helen Marymont became ill with stomach pains and bowel upsets, on and off. She went to the base doctor, who prescribed various medicaments, but there was no significant improvement, and she told the doctor that his remedies seemed to be doing her 'more harm than good'. She became moody and depressed and added concern about her health to her other worries. She asked her husband to send her home, but he told her that he could not afford it.

On 9 June 1958 Mrs Marymont attended a lunch party with nine other guests at the home of a friend in King's Lynn. After the meal she collapsed with stomach pains and diarrhoea so severe that she was rushed to hospital, where she died a few hours later. No one else who had attended the lunch party was taken ill, so food poisoning was ruled out. Since the woman's death was so sudden, her husband was routinely asked a number of questions by the hospital doctors. Had his wife had similar attacks on previous occasions? If so, when had they occurred, how long had they lasted, and what medical treatment had been prescribed? Did he know what had caused them? Asked whether he would object to a post-mortem, Marymont told his questioners that he most definitely did object, but he was overruled. Professor Francis Camps, the Home Office pathologist, was called upon to carry it out.

A police forensic expert, Dr Lewis Nickolls, examined the organs, and his findings were that Mrs Marymont had ingested a lethal dose of arsenic – at least three grains – about 24 hours before her death. He also discovered that she had taken at least two other doses on previous occasions; not enough to kill but enough to make her very sick. One dose must have been taken at least six months previous to her death, Dr Nickolls said. Arsenic has an affinity for keratin (the main constituent of hair) and the date of ingesting arsenic can be calculated against the rate of hair growth. As hair grows, it does not lose the arsenic it contains, and this shows in bands across the keratinous tissue. Mrs Marymont's hair showed the presence of a wide band near the roots and several narrower bands along its length and near the ends. The dates could be determined from the rate of hair growth when the arsenic had been administered, and these coincided with the dates on which Mrs Marymont had suffered her previous stomach and bowel attacks.

Once the forensic evidence had established arsenic as the cause of death, Camps told the court that the poison could easily be given in a cup of some strongly flavoured drink such as coffee or cocoa, which would mask the taste. He ruled out suicide, because no would-be suicide would choose such a painful and slow way to die.

The evidence pointing to Master Sergeant Marcus Marymont as the poisoner of his wife laid a trail as obvious as a line of pebbles in a wood to prevent someone losing his way. Not only was there the background of his passion for the other woman and his desire to marry her, which was common knowledge at the base, but also the airman had been incredibly indiscreet in his attempts to obtain arsenic. In Maidenhead he went into a chemist's shop and asked the assistant whether they sold arsenic. Told that he would need to sign the poisons register, he demurred. The request was in itself such an unusual one that the chemist's assistant remembered the occasion and had a very clear memory of what the potential customer looked like, and that he had been wearing US Air Force uniform at the time.

Again, he had drawn attention to himself by strolling casually into the US Air Force Laboratory after all the staff had left for the night, and handled a number of bottles on the shelves. Many of the bottles contained deadly drugs,

but there was no security and anyone in uniform could
have gone in and handled them – the door to the laboratory
was not even locked! Marymont spoke to a cleaner during
this visit, and on handling one bottle he mentioned the
subject of arsenic. The cleaner remembered this at the
subsequent trial, saying that the incident was so unusual
that it 'stuck in her mind' and, in particular, she remembered a jocular remark he made about arsenic, saying that
'someone would not need to take much of that if they
wished to bump themselves off'.

Cynthia Taylor, whom Marymont loved so desperately
that he was prepared to commit murder in order to make
her his wife, may have gone into the affair with her eyes
open, but she had certainly not expected to go through the
traumatic experience of testifying in court when justice
finally caught up with her homicidal lover. Marymont had
kept all her letters – there were some seventy or eighty of
them – in his quarters at the base, and they were read out in
all their graphic detail at the subsequent trial. What caused
her most anguish, however, was the knowledge that he
had lied to her all along that his wife and family were in the
States, even though he had been living with them on the
base all the time. She was not amused by the jibes of
Marymont's messmates either – in particular the favourite
comment that 'a soldier shouldn't tinker with a Taylor,
or he'll be in trouble'. This play on the popular rhyme
distressed her very much.

Just one month after the death of his wife, Marcus
Marymont was arrested and charged with her murder. The
trial lasted ten days, and his mother flew in from America to
give evidence of his hitherto unblemished character, and of
his award for gallantry during the war when he rescued a
sailor from a blazing ship. Asked about his three children,
he said that 'they were old enough not to need him', and he
reiterated his desire to marry Mrs Taylor when the divorce
she had applied for was granted.

But it was not to be. After 5½ hours' deliberation, a jury
of his peers found him guilty of murder, and he was
sentenced to life imprisonment, which was later reduced to
thirty-five years' penal servitude. When his unit returned

to America, he served the remainder of his sentence in a
Kansas gaol, and Cynthia Taylor was left with only her
memories.

9

The Suicide that Wasn't

Frederick Emmett-Dunne (1953)

Another soldier is the subject of this story – not an American this time but a British sergeant in the Royal Electrical and Mechanical Engineers (REME) based at Duisburg in Germany. By 1953 the British Army of Occupation of the Rhine (usually known as BAOR) had been established for some time. Its being peacetime, life at the base was easygoing, with the usual round of social activities, parties and so on, and there was a good deal of what came to be known as 'fraternization' – a somewhat euphemistic term for mixing with the German civilian population, in particular the girls. Judging from the number of marriages between British soldiers and German girls, this did not seem to be discouraged by the Army Authorities.

One such soldier who had married one of the local fräuleins was Reginald Watters, known as 'Tich' because he was only five feet tall. A Yorkshireman, he was a sergeant on the staff of the REME technical training unit at the Duisburg base.

Although Watters was frequently the butt of his colleagues' jokes on account of his diminutive size, he seemed to take it all in good part, and was friendly and outgoing – the life and soul of any party. He was rather partial to alcohol, yet even with his frequent hangovers he was still cheerful and never known to become morose or maudlin, much less aggressive. It was therefore somewhat surprising to find that his best buddy was a man so different from him in every way as to invite comment from those closest to him.

Watters's friend was Frederick Emmett-Dunne (known as 'Mick'), a six-foot Irishman, who became a REME sergeant after having previously served in the Royal Marines and seen action in North Africa with the Irish Guards. Taken prisoner there, he had been struck in the back with a rifle butt by a German guard, causing a permanent injury. He had also received injuries to both legs later in his Army career when a Bren-gun shell exploded on a training exercise. Despite these mishaps, however, he always averred that he enjoyed army life and would not change it for any other.

Emmett-Dunne was not as popular as his pint-sized friend. For one thing, he was openly suspected of misappropriating regimental funds, although this was never proved. He was also quick to take offence – 'he had a short fuse,' one of his messmates said. And he had little compunction in paying attentions to married women – and to Mia Watters in particular.

Rumours were rife in the sergeants' mess. It was hinted darkly that Mia Watters and Frederick Emmett-Dunne 'got along like wildfire,' as one man put it. Vague allusions were made in the course of after-drinks chat at the social gatherings of the NCOs' wives. It was even said that Mia and Emmett-Dunne were meeting outside the normal round of social occasions. It soon came to the attention of Watters that something must be going on, on the principle that there's no smoke without fire. Mia Watters denied any romantic involvement with Emmett-Dunne, but admitted that she frequently danced with him at the base social functions because he was a very good dancer and she preferred to enjoy a decent dance than to have her 'feet trodden on by every clumsy Tom, Dick or Harry'. Watters was not a keen dancer himself, and had told his wife that he did not mind her dancing with other men; but an assortment of dancing-partners was one thing, and monopolizing one man at a dance was another. It seems that jealousy was already beginning to raise its ugly head.

Asked at a later stage about evidence that he frequently drove past the Watterses' quarters and that Mia followed a few moments later in her own car, Emmett-Dunne said that this was not true, as also was the story that he had been seen driving along the autobahn with Mrs Watters in the passenger seat. He also denied telling a girl he dated that he was in love with a married woman.

Things reached the point where Watters felt impelled to confide in one of the quartermaster-sergeants who was one of his close friends. He said that he thought 'some fishy business' was going on between his wife and Emmett-Dunne. He thought it strange, for one thing, that the Irishman called at his quarters every Sunday afternoon with the newspapers, when he (Watters) was perfectly capable of collecting them himself. The point was that Mia was always in on Sunday afternoons, whereas her husband was not. The quartermaster-sergeant later said that Watters seemed quite upset when relating his suspicions. 'His jealousy had become an obsession,' he added.

About a month later, on 30 November 1953, Watters, who was intending to sell his car, left his quarters at about 7 p.m. to meet a potential buyer. His wife expected him home by about eight o'clock, and when he did not return she asked two friends to go and look for him so that the meal she was cooking for their supper would not be spoiled. The two soldiers found him – hanging by the neck from the banisters in the entrance to No. 3 Block of the barracks. A bucket on which the sergeant had apparently stood lay on its side nearby. One of the soldiers went to telephone for assistance, and when he came back to the scene he found Emmett-Dunne leaning against a wall vomiting. The body had been cut down and was lying on the floor covered by a gas cape. When Emmett-Dunne had recovered, he said, 'My God, he has done it. I've cut him down. He was still making gurgling noises, even though he was dead. That made me as sick as a dog.'

The suicide – for such it was assumed to be – of the diminutive sergeant was so unexpected that it caused a sensation in Duisburg army circles. It was completely out of character, many said, for a man so outgoing and happy-go-lucky. If he had harboured any resentment about the partiality of his wife for his friend, he kept it to himself. He certainly did not talk about it in the sergeants' mess. Emmett-Dunne, however, was not averse to rumour-mongering, and he had been heard on one occasion to hint darkly that 'if somebody's wife didn't behave herself her husband would probably kill himself when he found out'. No one, however, took him seriously, even if they twigged whose wife he was referring to.

Thirty-six hours after Watters was found hanging, Dr Alan Womack, an Army pathologist attached to the British forces in Germany, carried out a post-mortem. He found that the thyroid cartilage had been fractured, and that there was bruising of the larynx and trachea, as well as the throat muscles. After examining the battered and discoloured neck, Dr Womack found that the furrow left by the rope used in the hanging was situated higher up the neck than the various injuries above described. He found no other injuries on the body, but he did find that a meal had been ingested about an hour or so before death, and he considered it somewhat unusual for a man contemplating suicide to eat a meal first. Although the case bore some puzzling features, the Army court felt that a verdict of suicide was the only feasible one.

Despite the court's findings, the rumours started flying around more noisily than buzzing bees. Scarcely anyone on the base, nor the German civilians employed there, believed that Watters had committed suicide; they thought that someone had 'bumped him off' and that it was a put-up job, a faked suicide, and they were not averse to saying so. Lieutenant-Colonel Frank Elliott, Assistant Provost-Marshal of the Special Investigation Department, was on leave at the time, but on his return he felt that further probing into the matter was in order. He applied to the Metropolitan Police, who sent Detective Superintendent Colin MacDougal to render him all the assistance necessary.

The two senior officers and their assistants were experienced detectives, and on the available evidence they were certainly of the opinion that there was more to the apparent suicide of Sergeant Watters than met the eye. First of all, the injuries to the throat of the dead soldier, they surmised, seemed far more severe than could have been caused simply by hanging alone; it seemed to them that such injuries were more consistent with a blow, such as a person with a knowledge of unarmed combat such as ju-jitsu could inflict with the side of the hand. Consultations and experiments were held at the London headquarters of the Judo Club, after which further experiments were carried out at the military hospital in Hostert, in Germany. The aim of these consultations and experiments was mainly to ascertain how vertical fractures of the thyroid cartilage could be caused.

These preliminary investigations were merely the forerunners of the revelations which were to surface some six months after the death of Watters, during which time even more eyebrows were raised and tongues were wagging at the Duisburg base when the news reached those living there that Emmett-Dunne, who had been posted to Catterick in the mean time, had married Mia Watters in England.

The news also reached Ronald Emmett, a half-brother of Emmett-Dunne, who had served in the same unit with him in Duisburg at the time of Watters's death, but who was now back in civilian life and living in Cheshire. The half-buried suspicions he had had at the time now surfaced more strongly, and his conscience was troubled. Finding himself unable to live with the nagging doubts, he decided to communicate with the police at Hoylake, Cheshire, who passed on the information he gave them to the Army authorities. Emmett-Dunne was arrested and taken to Bow Street Magistrates' Court in London and charged with murder. The news that Watters's body had been exhumed shook him visibly.

The military authorities at this point took over and flew the prisoner to Bielefeld, where the military corrective establishment was situated. Charged with murdering Watters, Emmett-Dunne was court-martialled before eight members of the Army's judicial system under Brigadier D. L. Betts, with a civilian lawyer to give guidance on points of law.

The second post-mortem on the exhumed body of Watters was carried out by Professor Francis Camps, the renowned pathologist from the Home Office, who flew out to the military cemetery in Cologne. The body was identified by a signet ring which Watters had always worn. Camps made an exhaustive examination of the larynx and trachea as well as the thyroid cartilage, cricoid bone and other tissues of the throat area, and removed the larynx for microscopical investigation in the laboratory.

Mr Griffith-Jones, prosecuting, asked Camps whether Watters could have died as a result of hanging; Camps's reply was a most emphatic 'no'.

'In your opinion, what *did* he die from?' the prosecutor asked. 'In my view,' replied the pathologist, 'he died from shock caused by a blow to the neck.'

There was no doubt that Emmett-Dunne knew just how to kill a man by a chopping blow with the side of the hand, with elbow raised. The accused was known to be an expert at ju-jitsu and karate. It now remained to be shown that Watters had in fact been killed by such a blow, that the prisoner at the bar was the man who had dealt it, and that afterwards the body had been hanged in order to fake a suicide. Just merely proving that the accused had the knowledge of, and expertise in, unarmed combat did not automatically prove that he was the man who had killed Watters in this manner.

It was at this point that Ronald Emmett, the accused's half-brother, gave the dramatic evidence that would show up the supposed suicide for what it was – a hollow sham. He said that on the night Watters was found dead his brother had sent a soldier to look for him – he served in the same unit – and bring him to where Emmett-Dunne was waiting for him, in the entrance to No.3 Block of the barracks. When he arrived, he said that Emmett-Dunne was 'shaking like a leaf' and he asked him what had happened. 'What's up, old boy?' was how he put it.

'Don't you old boy me!' his brother had retorted. 'I've just killed a man, that's what! We had an argument, I just gave him a tap and now he's dead. My God! What am I going to do?'

'What was it all about?' Ronald asked.

'He was having a go at me,' his brother replied. 'He came up to me and told me to keep away from his wife. I told him not to talk so bloody stupid. Then he came towards me in a threatening sort of way, so I pushed him and he fell.'

'Did he strike you first?'

'No . . . no. I just didn't have the time or the inclination to argue – I didn't want to know. So I just gave him a tap to shut him up.'

Ronald then told the court that his brother asked him what he ought to do, and as he walked around behind the staircase where the body lay to show him, he spotted a coil of rope lying on the floor. 'We'll hang him up from the banisters', he had suggested, 'to make it look like he hanged himself.' He then looked for an object to place near the feet of the hanging body, and found a tin bucket, which he up-ended a few feet away as though it had been kicked away by the 'suicide' and rolled over.

Emmett-Dunne then told Ronald to get into his car and leave the scene before anyone saw them, adding, 'Don't forget that you are my brother.'

Mr Derek Curtis-Bennett, who defended Emmett-Dunne, then asked the accused: 'Was the idea of hanging the body a mutual idea?' Ronald's answer to this question was an unhesitating 'No, sir.'

In his cross-examination of Ronald Emmett, Mr Curtis-Bennett asked him why he had suddenly decided to go to the police at Hoylake with his story so long after the events had taken place. 'Was it because you were frightened that you might be involved?' he said.

'No,' Ronald replied. 'Up to the moment I read about the marriage [of Emmett-Dunne and Mia Watters] I had believed it was an accident. When I read about the marriage, I began to think it might not have been an accident after all . . .'

Frederick Emmett-Dunne was sentenced to death by hanging and did not appeal, but he petitioned the Queen for mercy (a choice open only to a member of Her Majesty's Armed Forces) and his petition was rejected. He did not hang, however, since capital punishment had been abolished in Germany, and his sentence was commuted to one of life imprisonment.

And Mia? The passion for which he killed must have

been more on his side than on hers, for she quickly found herself another man. In 1964, while Emmett-Dunne was in prison, he was granted a divorce on the grounds of his wife's adultery, after which she lost no time in marrying the new boyfriend who, like her ex-husband, was also an Englishman, though not a soldier.

10

A Deadly Bedside Manner

Dr Hawley Harvey Crippen (1910)

No one, seeing the meek-looking, mild-mannered little
man in the dock of the Old Bailey, would ever have thought
him capable of murder as he peered over the rail at his
accusers through his gold-rimmed spectacles. Several
inches short of even average height, he appeared taller
because of his high, bald forehead, and he looked older
than his forty-eight years owing to his heavy sandy moustache which, together with his baldness, gave him the
benevolent look of the kind of elderly man one so often sees
taking his grandchildren and the dog out for a walk in
the park. Without exception, all the witnesses at his
trial described him as kindly, gentle, well-mannered. A
murderer? Impossible, they said. But let us start at the
beginning.

Hawley Harvey Crippen was born in Michigan, USA, in
1862, and completed his education at college in order to
pursue medical studies. He qualified as a doctor with the
award of a diploma from the faculty of the Medical College
of Philadelphia, and subsequently obtained another
diploma as an eye-and-ear specialist from the Ophthalmic
Hospital in New York City in 1885. He then practised in
several of the larger American cities.

While he was practising in New York he met a girl of
seventeen named Cora Turner – a name she had adopted as
being much easier to spell and pronounce than her original
name of Kunigunde Mackamotzki, derived from her first-
generation-immigrant parentage – her mother was German, her father a Polish Jew. Cora's chief preoccupation, it
seemed, was the furtherance of her chosen career of opera
singer, and when the little doctor proposed marriage and

agreed to pay for her voice to be trained at a New York musical academy, she was delighted.

In 1900 the doctor, with his young wife, decided to come to England, where he had been offered a post as manager of the offices of Munyon's, a patent medicine company, in Shaftesbury Avenue in London's West End. Forced to abandon her singing lessons at the New York academy, Cora now decided to seek engagements singing on the music-hall stage – a far cry from grand opera, but her voice was not, perhaps, in the same class as Dame Nellie Melba after all. She called herself Belle Elmore, which she considered sounded much more suitable for the stage than Cora Crippen.

At this time the couple lived in South Crescent, off Tottenham Court Road, and in 1902 his firm's head office in Philadelphia recalled him for six months. During her husband's absence, Cora stayed at their London home, avidly pursuing as many engagements as she was able to obtain on the music-hall stage, supplemented by some concerts in the larger and better-class pubs, known as 'smoking-room concerts'. It was at one of these functions that Cora met an American music-hall performer named Bruce Miller and, if her husband's version is to be believed, saw rather more of him than the doctor would have liked.

On Crippen's return from the States they took up residence at a house in Store Street, Bloomsbury. Munyon's had also moved their London premises to Albion House, New Oxford Street. In the same building was an American dental firm called Yale Tooth Specialists, and Crippen was soon entering into a partnership with the proprietor of this firm as a sideline to his main occupation as manager of Munyon's. Needing a secretary, he employed a typist named Ethel le Neve, whom he had met some time previously at the Drouet Institute. Finally, he took over Munyon's London branch on commission as a franchise, but he found that in this form he could not make the company a viable concern, and so after sixteen years' association with the firm he terminated his connection with it in January 1910.

The loss of his job was ill-timed, for he had just purchased a house on lease at 39 Hilldrop Crescent in Camden Town. They economized by dispensing with a maid, doing their own domestic work. In the meantime Cora – or Belle Elmore – was becoming more well known and popular as a music-hall singer, mostly in London but occasionally in suburban venues. She also became honorary treasurer of the Music Hall Ladies' Guild, with headquarters in Albion House – the same building as her husband's erstwhile business ventures. She was described by her contemporaries as vivacious and pleasant, with more than a streak of vanity – fond of dress and display. She dyed her dark hair auburn, and spent lavishly on such items as jewellery and furs.

Unfortunately, as her husband's resources dwindled and Cora's own fortunes improved, her natural ebullience and vitality degenerated into a coarse vulgarity and loudness of manner. She took over the running of the household, and there is no doubt that the mild-mannered little doctor was henpecked to a degree. He was forced to do the domestic work while his wife held the purse-strings and even chose his suits and ties. Much against his wishes, Cora took in several lodgers, and also imported a French maid whose main duties were to serve meals and drinks when Cora entertained her theatrical friends. While putting on an act of politeness during these parties, Cora let all restraint go as soon as her guests had left the house, and let fly at her uncomplaining spouse with belittlement and abuse.

It was perhaps inevitable that Crippen should seek solace elsewhere as a refuge from the well-nigh intolerable conditions at home, but it was not until five years after their first meeting that Ethel le Neve became his mistress. It cannot be denied that the doctor had a genuine love and affection as well as passion for his secretary; this was no mere fleeting infatuation. For three years, once their mutual attraction had culminated in their final surrender to the upsurge of feeling that engulfed them, their liaison continued with their meeting in obscure hotel bedrooms after office hours.

On the last day of January 1910 the Crippens were hosts to a theatrical couple, the Martinettis. Dinner was served, after which Crippen invited all to join in a game of whist in

the parlour. Mrs Martinetti helped her friend Belle Elmore
in the kitchen (the maid had been given a day off) and they
took a tray of drinks into the parlour to enjoy during the
game. At 1.30 in the morning the Martinettis left to walk
home, the buses having all stopped running, and their last
recollection of that evening was of their hosts waving
goodbye to them from the top of the steps leading from the
front door of 39 Hilldrop Crescent down to the deserted
lamplit street. 'Don't bother to come down, Belle,' Mrs
Martinetti said. 'You don't want to catch your death of
cold.' Her remark was prophetic, but it was not a cold that
caused it . . .

The next day – or perhaps we should call it the same day,
since it was not until 1.30 a.m. that the Martinettis had
taken their leave – Crippen called at their flat in Shaftesbury
Avenue to inquire after Mr Martinetti, who had expressed a
feeling of indisposition the previous evening.

'Thank you, I feel a lot better today,' he had replied,
adding, 'And how is Belle?'

'Oh, she's OK,' Crippen said.

At this point Mrs Martinetti appeared with a cup of tea
and asked Crippen to give Belle her love.

'I'll certainly do that,' Crippen replied, and after enjoying
the tea and indulging in small-talk about the weather and
suchlike topics, he took his leave.

The next day saw Crippen pawning one of his wife's
diamond rings and a pair of earrings for £80 – a considerable
sum in 1910 – and that night Ethel le Neve spent the night at
39 Hilldrop Crescent. She expressed surprise that Mrs
Crippen was not at home. 'Oh, she's had to go at short
notice to America,' was his plausible explanation. 'Her
brother's been taken seriously ill and is not expected to
live.'

On 3 February the Music Hall Ladies' Guild secretary and
chairman each received a letter dated 2 February tendering
Mrs Crippen's resignation of her honorary treasurer's position, with the explanation that the serious illness of a near
relative had summoned her to the United States at short
notice. The letters were not Belle's handwriting.

Mrs Martinetti heard of her friend's precipitate departure

for America only at second hand from a member of the Ladies' Guild, and did not hesitate to take the doctor to task for being so remiss as not to inform her personally, in view of the fact that she and Belle were close friends. There were profuse apologies, along with the plausible excuses. He had been so busy, he said, packing his wife's trunks, finding out the sailing schedules of the ships, and calling a cab to get Belle to the docks, that it had taken them all night, and he had clean forgotten to notify her. Mrs Martinetti thought it a bit odd, but she said nothing.

Later that month Crippen pawned more rings and a diamond and ruby clip for a total of £115, and on the 20th he took Ethel le Neve to the Music Hall Ladies' Guild ball, staged by the Guild's Benevolent Fund Committee. Miss le Neve was seen to be openly wearing another diamond clip as well as earrings, rings and other jewellery known to be the property of Belle Elmore. There was a good deal of gossip among the Guild members about this, and plenty of snide remarks were bandied about, the gist of which was that the doctor was 'a dark horse', and that 'while the cat's away the mice will play'.

On 12 March Ethel gave up her secretarial job and came to live at 39 Hilldrop Crescent, ostensibly as the doctor's housekeeper and live-in secretary-clerk. Just before Easter he told Mrs Martinetti that he had heard from Belle's relatives in America that she was very ill and not expected to recover, and that if she died he would take a week's holiday in France. Mrs Martinetti and Belle's other thespian friends thought all this sounded very odd indeed . . .

On 24 March, which was Maundy Thursday, Mrs Martinetti received the following telegram:

BELLE DIED YESTERDAY AT SIX O'CLOCK =
= CRIPPEN =

The telegram had been sent from Victoria Station, just before Crippen and Ethel le Neve set off for Dieppe. While they were on holiday in France, an obituary notice appeared in the *Era*.

On his return, Crippen fended off all attempts to send

wreaths, letters of condolence and other tokens by Belle's friends. He said that such items would arrive too late, as Belle had already been cremated and the ashes were being sent to England. For a bereaved husband, it was observed that Crippen was apparently exhibiting no marked signs of distress, and was his usual calm and composed self. He carried on with his normal day-to-day activities, visiting the Martinettis and other friends and leaving his home daily for Albion House, where he still had some working connections with Yale Tooth Specialists. Ethel ran the house efficiently, combining this with her duties in the doctor's office, but it was observed that she was now quite openly wearing Belle's furs as well as her jewellery.

Crippen must have considered himself safe from any awkward investigations into his wife's apparent death in America, despite the fact that gossip was rife about his living with Ethel le Neve in the same house and that the girl was wearing his late wife's accoutrements. But he had not reckoned with the persistent curiosity and scepticism of a Mr Nash, who had been a friend of his wife, and who had occasion to make a short visit to the United States. While he was there, having been primed with the names and addresses of several of Belle's relatives, friends and acquaintances in America, he made a series of inquiries. He was quite unsuccessful in obtaining any news at all of her alleged last days, and he was told that, as far as these persons knew, Belle had not been back to the States at all since she had gone to England as Dr Crippen's bride. Thoroughly perturbed, Nash returned to England and bearded the lion in his den. Receiving no believable replies from the doctor, Nash took his suspicions to Scotland Yard.

The famous Chief Inspector Dew – made so by this case – was sent to interview Crippen at his office in Albion House. Although Crippen must have been inwardly quaking with fright, his superb powers of self-control stood him in good stead as he cooked up yet another story calculated to persuade the detectives that he had no hand in his wife's disappearance, as Nash had darkly hinted. Crippen began disarmingly by admitting that he had told everyone a pack of lies in order to avoid the scandal that would have ensued if he had told them the truth – that Belle had left him and eloped with her American friend Bruce Miller. Dew asked Crippen if he would mind his house being searched – he had a search warrant – and the doctor told him to go ahead. The Chief Inspector went through every room from the attic to the coal-cellar, but found nothing. He had by the end of the day been persuaded that the little doctor was telling him the truth.

If Crippen had realized this, and had stood his ground, he might possibly have remained beyond suspicion. But he did what so many murderers have done both before and since – he panicked. Hastily he bought a set of boy's clothing to fit Ethel le Neve, who was enjoined to put up her hair into a man's cap, pulled well down over her face, and not to talk to anyone lest her feminine voice betray her, and the pair set sail for Antwerp, from where they took ship for North America. No one had watched them – they were not under suspicion. Only when Chief Inspector Dew called at 39 Hilldrop Crescent two days later, merely to check the small detail of a date, and found the place deserted and the doctor and his mistress gone, did he realize that he had been conned. It was galling, of course, to admit it, even to himself; but he did not let this stop him launching an all-out search. Only a guilty man, he reasoned, would flee – and so precipitately at that.

Every policeman in Britain was on the look-out for the doctor and his slender young companion – at that stage no one, of course, knew that she was disguised as a boy. Dew and his men decided to give the deserted house in Hilldrop Crescent another and more thorough going-over. Every room was subjected to the minutest scrutiny, and even the garden was dug up, but nothing suspicious was found until the third day of the search, when Dew noticed that a few bricks in the floor of the coal-cellar seemed to be loose. He instructed his men to lift the loose bricks, and as they were being prised up the nostrils of the diggers were assailed by an unpleasant and unmistakable odour, despite the layer of lime which had been sprinkled in an effort to mask it. Buried not far beneath the surface were the remains of Belle

Elmore. It was 13 July – a day which would in due course prove to be very unlucky for somebody.

Police were still looking for Crippen and Ethel le Neve while an autopsy was being carried out on what was left of the unfortunate Belle Elmore. Four pathologists worked on the autopsy: Dr William Wilcox and Dr A. P. Luff analysed the various organs, while Dr (later Sir) Bernard Spilsbury, assisted by Dr A. J. Pepper, devoted their attention to the skin, in particular to an operation scar on the abdomen which was to prove crucial to the identification of the body. The case was to make Spilsbury's reputation.

*   *   *

On 16 July a warrant was issued for the arrest of Hawley Harvey Crippen and Ethel le Neve. The police description of Ethel credited her with having a 'nice-looking, pleasant ladylike appearance'. Chief Inspector Dew, who compiled the 'wanted for murder' poster, is unlikely to have described her thus could he have seen her in her ill-fitting male garb. But the remainder of his description – slender, five feet five inchs tall, pale-faced, with light brown hair and large grey-blue eyes – fitted her to a T, although the light brown hair had been bundled unceremoniously into a man's cap. Dew's description of Crippen was also not quite up to date, since Crippen had shaved off his moustache.

The first ship for the American continent from Antwerp when the couple arrived there was bound for Canada, and they boarded her without delay. The ss *Montrose* set sail for Quebec on 20 July. After a couple of hours out on the Atlantic the captain, who had read the description of the fugitives in the English newspapers and had heard it on the radio, became suspicious of two of his passengers, a Mr John Robinson and his son John. The youth, said to be sixteen, was attired in a suit too big for him – so much too big that it had been taken in with safety-pins. Someone could not sew, that was for sure. The boy always wore his cap pulled right down over his face, and his feet, shod in white canvas shoes, seemed very small and dainty, even for a sixteen-year-old boy. And another thing: the father and son seemed to display a great deal more affection in public than he, Captain Kendall, considered usual. They were always holding hands, even squeezing each other's fingers, and walking about on deck with their arms around one another's waists.

Two days later, after observing the couple's comportment closely and referring again to the newspapers he had with him, Captain Kendall sent the famous wireless telegraphic message to Scotland Yard – the first time wireless telegraphy had ever been used in pursuit of a fugitive from justice by the captain of a ship at sea. Dew made arrangements for the ship to be intercepted before she docked, and for the next eleven days Mr John Robinson and his son John had the freedom of the deck in blissful ignorance, huddling together to make plans for a new life in the United States, where they would make their way from Canada. A new home, a new job, and forget about Chief Inspector Dew.

But Chief Inspector Dew was not so easily to be forgotten. On Sunday, 31 July, the ship was steaming slowly up the St Lawrence River towards Quebec, when at about 9 a.m. a pilot boat came alongside. Dew was aboard, having sailed on 23 July from Liverpool on a faster ship, the ss *Laurentic*. 'Mr Robinson' was on the deck, enjoying the sight of land and doubtless rejoicing in the anticipation of safety and a new life; his 'son John' was in Cabin No. 5, curled up on the bunk reading a novel.

Dew came aboard and was escorted straight to the bridge, where he met Captain Kendall. Looking down on the deck below, he spotted Crippen, unmistakable despite the absence of the familiar moustache.

Dew descended the companion-way. 'Good-morning, Dr Crippen,' he said quietly. 'I am Chief Inspector Walter Dew, of Scotland Yard.'

'Good-morning, Mr Dew,' he replied. 'You've come a long way.'

Crippen was formally arrested and charged with the murder of his wife.

Dew then went to Cabin No. 5. 'Miss le Neve?' he inquired. 'I am Chief Inspector Dew . . .'

She took one look at the Yard man and fainted.

Crippen told Dew: 'I'm not sorry you've found me – the anxiety has been too much. I am glad to get it over with. But it is only fair to tell you that Ethel knows nothing about it – she had no part in it. I never told her anything.'

Another wireless telegraphic message now went to Scotland Yard – this time from Dew instead of to him. It read simply:

> **CRIPPEN AND LE NEVE ARRESTED =**
> **= DEW =**

Dew returned to England triumphantly with his two prisoners, boarding a Liverpool-bound ship from a tug off Montreal. Huge crowds booed and jeered the couple as they arrived at the Liverpool docks, and again at Euston when they arrived in London. They were sent for trial at the Old Bailey.

The trial of Hawley Harvey Crippen opened on 18 October 1910 before the Lord Chief Justice, Lord Alverstone. Crippen was defended by Mr A. A. Tobin, KC, later to become a judge; his juniors were Mr Huntly Jenkins and Mr Roome. The prosecutor was Mr Richard Muir. The trial lasted five days, and the Crown witnesses on the first day included the Martinettis, Bruce Miller, Cora Crippen's sister (both of whom arrived from America to appear as witnesses), several of Crippen's business acquaintances and associates, both American and English, and several friends of the couple. The second day was taken up by Chief Inspector Dew's evidence, and on the third day the crucial evidence of the forensic pathologists began, on which the whole outcome of the trial would depend.

Dr Pepper was the first to step into the arena. He described the portion of abdominal skin bearing an old operation scar, and he went on to say that the evisceration of the body had been carried out by a person skilled in dissection and fully conversant with human anatomy. He said that the remains, which were devoid of a head, bones or limbs, were those of a middle-aged adult, probably female. A tuft of dark hair which had been dyed auburn with henna was also found, and this pointed to a female victim, as also did the presence of a lady's vest in the makeshift grave.

During cross-examination this scar was hotly debated. Opposing counsel's medical witnesses insisted that it was not a scar but a fold in the skin caused by the position of the body in its cramped grave. It was at this point that Spilsbury came to the rescue with his expert findings. Describing his critical microscopic examination of the section of skin, he stated that it was one and a half inches in length and nearly half an inch wide, and at each end of the mark he found glands, but there were none in its centre. This proved, he averred, that the mark was a scar and not a fold in the skin. It was also known that Cora Crippen had undergone an abdominal operation shortly before her marriage to Crippen.

Perhaps this was why the defence was so anxious to refute the suggestion that the mark was a scar. They were strenuously attempting to show that the remains had been buried in the coal-cellar of 39 Hilldrop Crescent *before* the Crippens had taken occupation, and that they were not necessarily those of a woman. The presence of a woman's vest meant nothing, they insisted; a man's pyjama jacket had also been found there, and the person who had buried the body could have just taken whatever garments were readily to hand to wrap the remains. However, the notion that an unidentified body had been buried in the house earlier was soon scotched when a painstaking investigation revealed that the pyjamas to which the jacket belonged could not have been purchased before the Crippens had moved in. They were to a design sold by Jones Bros. of Holloway only after the end of 1908, whereas the Crippens had moved to 39 Hilldrop Crescent on 21 September 1905. In those days it was commonplace for shops to deliver goods to the customer's address rather than the purchaser paying for them and taking them with him, and records at Jones Bros. showed that three identical pyjama suits were supplied to Dr Crippen in January 1909, all of the new pattern. When the house was searched initially by Dew and his men, two pairs of these pyjamas were found together with the trousers of a third pair, which matched the jacket found in the grave in the coal-cellar.

The trial went relentlessly into its fourth day, and the

pathologists who had examined the remains described their findings of hyoscine, an alkaloid poison, in the organs. A more than fatal dose – 2.7 grains of the poison – was found to be present, which, given to the unsuspecting victim in a cup of tea or coffee, would have immediately made her drowsy and she would have fallen into a deep sleep within an hour – a sleep from which there would be no awakening. Death would have ensued within, at the most, ten to twelve hours.

It was known that Dr Crippen had ordered five grains of hyoscine from Lewis & Burrows, the New Oxford Street chemists, on 17 January. There was no difficulty in supplying such a deadly narcotic to a doctor, but it was an unusually large amount to order at one time, and the firm had to obtain it from the wholesalers. Crippen received it on 19 January, having signed the poisons register. This was the only time that Crippen had ever purchased hyoscine during his entire medical career, and it was also the first time that the drug had ever been used to murder a person in British criminal history.

By the time the fifth day of the trial was drawing to a close, all the additional circumstantial evidence put forward seemed superfluous, such as the fact that Belle Elmore's cabin trunk full of clothes, and her fox and ermine furs, had been left in the house together with various items of jewellery. If Belle had really eloped to America with Bruce Miller, the prosecution pointed out, it is hardly likely that she would have left behind such items – Belle was, by all accounts, a vain woman inordinately fond of personal adornment. Crippen had pawned, rather than sold, only a few items from the collection of jewellery – just enough to raise the money to get himself and Ethel le Neve to Canada. All this was ammunition in the prosecution's gun, but it did little to further the case, the outcome of which had been a foregone conclusion from the forensic evidence alone.

The jury were out for only 27 minutes before returning a verdict of guilty of murder, and Crippen was sentenced to death. 'I still protest my innocence, my lord,' was his reply when the judge asked him whether he wished to say anything before sentence, in the usual way. On 5

November Crippen's appeal against his conviction was dismissed by the Court of Criminal Appeal, and he was hanged in Pentonville on 23 November 1910.

Shortly before his execution he wrote a last letter to Ethel le Neve, part of which read:

> There are less than two days left to us. Only one more letter after this can I write to you, and only two more visits . . . Your letter written early Saturday came to me last Saturday-evening, and soon after the Governor brought me the dreadful news about ten o'clock. When he had gone I kissed your face in the photo . . .

Crippen's last request was that all Ethel's letters and photographs be buried with him, which was granted.

In the mean time, the unfortunate Belle Elmore had been buried in the cemetery in Finchley, and the trial of Ethel le Neve, on the charge of being an accessory after the fact, commenced on 25 October, two days after Crippen's trial had ended. The same judge and the same prosecutor officiated; Ethel was defended by Mr F. E. Smith, KC (afterwards Lord Birkenhead). The trial lasted less than a day, and she was not called upon to give any evidence; she was acquitted and freed. She was twenty-seven, but owing to her youthful and slender appearance, she had easily been able to pass for sixteen in her days as a 'boy' on board ship. Now, however, in court, she was dressed all in black and heavily veiled, and had resumed the 'pleasant ladylike appearance' which Dew had bestowed upon her in his description.

It is not known with absolute certainty what happened to this ill-starred lover of the little doctor – he was only five feet three inches – who had given her his heart and poisoned the virago of a wife with whom he was encumbered so that he could marry her. There are a number of conflicting stories as to her subsequent career. I have studied all these carefully, and have come to the conclusion that the most likely version is that she emigrated to the United States, where she died in 1950.

11

For Love of a Gypsy

Charlotte Bryant (1935)

The story of the two lovers of this chapter is a very different one from that of Crippen and Ethel le Neve, and the protagonists could not be more opposite to them in every way – the man coarse and brutish, the woman illiterate, habitually unkempt and frequently unwashed, even lousy. It is strange that any man, however uncouth himself, could be attracted to her. Still, as Yorkshire people say, there's nowt so queer as folk . . .

Charlotte Bryant was the wife of a corporal in the English military police, who met her when he was serving in Ireland during the 'Troubles' of 1920–21. The uneducated Irish peasant girl was nineteen at the time; Frederick Bryant was twenty-five. He brought his bride to England at the termination of his service, and they were married in March 1922.

Frederick Bryant soon found that discharged soldiers were a drug on the market. Unemployment was rife – and ex-soldiers were ten a penny. After spending a good deal of time looking round, and drawing the dole, he eventually found a job as a farm labourer in Somerset, at a place called Over Compton, near Yeovil. The farm was technically in Dorset, but in actuality (according to the Ordnance Survey map) it was situated just across the border with Somerset. There was a tied cottage with the job, an abundance of farm produce available, and the cottage had its own acre of garden to grow vegetables and keep chickens, a pig and even a cow. But the hours were long, even though the 'perks' made up in large measure for the low wages of an agricultural labourer.

It was a great disappointment, therefore, for Fred when

he discovered – as he soon did – that his wife was sluttish and lazy, and did not lift a finger in the house. She expected him to do all the domestic chores after a long and hard day out in the fields, while she betook herself to the local taverns. And it was not only drink that was the attraction – it was men, and a good many men at that. She soon acquired several opprobrious nicknames, such as 'Compton Liz' and 'Killarney Kate' – all intended to give the impression that she was little more than a part-time prostitute.

Fred decided to make the best of a bad job. His wife's earnings as a part-time harlot were useful to supplement his meagre wages, and at least they did not get into debt. As he looked round the dirty and dilapidated cottage that was his home, he reflected ruefully how he had been taken for a sucker, lumbering himself with a woman who was completely undomesticated and immoral to boot. What could he do? A divorce would cost money, although he had plenty of grounds. But he would never be able to afford one. He gritted his teeth, said very little and went back to his milking and haymaking and sheep-dipping.

In the eleven years from her marriage up to 1933, Charlotte Bryant bore five children, and it is pretty certain that the paternity of at least some of them was in doubt. But the amiable and complaisant Fred took them all in his stride and raised them all as his own.

Around Christmas of 1933 Charlotte met a gypsy pedlar and horse-dealer in one of the pubs she frequented. The pair took an instant liking to one another. He was crude, loud-mouthed and paid little more attention to hygiene and grooming than she did, so they were well suited. Eventually she told Fred that Leonard Parsons, the gypsy, ought to come and live with them as a lodger; the money would be useful, she pointed out, and more regular than the income from going 'on the game'. Fred agreed.

Leonard Parsons slept on an old couch in the kitchen, since there was no spare bedroom in the house; he did not mind, since he was away most of the time anyway selling things and horse-trading. When he was at home, however, he made the fullest use of the opportunities available to him, in the unprepossessing person of his landlord's wife.

Fred's uncomplaining complacency at this *ménage à trois* came to an abrupt end. The farmer who employed him was sick to death of the scandal caused in the neighbourhood by the goings-on at the cottage and his employee's wife's reputation in all the pubs in the immediate area. The farmer gave Fred the sack. A few miles away, however, at Coombe, near Sherborne in Dorset, another farmer badly needed a labourer, and he offered Fred the job, which also included a tied cottage, as did most jobs of this nature. It is unlikely that the farmer was unaware of the scandal, so it appears that he was less fussy than his predecessor and concerned only that his employee could do the work required.

Fred and Charlotte Bryant soon picked up the threads of their life again, Charlotte openly cohabiting with her gypsy lover, and Fred perhaps not relishing his role as the cuckolded husband but putting the family finances first. However, he began to look askance at the behaviour of his wife when Parsons put in his periodic reappearances at their home after his sojourns. She showed every sign of being completely besotted with her unshaven and unkempt gypsy lover, welcoming his returns with evident excitement, and telling her women friends that she was in love with him. At least she had given up the prostitution, and visited the pubs far less frequently these days.

More than once Charlotte went with Parsons on his travels, leaving her husband to look after the five children as best he could while doing a full-time job. Fred began to remonstrate with his wife more and more, telling her that enough was enough. He had to keep his job in order to live in the cottage – which was a much better one than their previous abode – and he could not do it properly and be responsible for feeding and changing babies too. That was woman's work, he pointed out. After a fourteen-hour day out in the fields, he did not feel much like washing, ironing or cooking, sweeping up or scrubbing floors either. Leaving piles of dirty clothes on the floor, unwashed dishes in the sink and a two-inch layer of dust over everything was not his idea of domestic life either.

Fred might have been talking to the wall. All Charlotte was interested in was her gypsy paramour. Something would have to be done: he would not be able to marry her if Fred could or would not divorce her, and she was getting fed up with his constant nagging. Yes, she would have to think of something . . .

On 14 May 1935, two years and five months after Parsons had started lodging with them, Fred Bryant was suddenly taken ill with acute stomach pains and vomiting. Charlotte called in the local doctor, a Dr McCarthy, who diagnosed gastro-enteritis. Fred was of robust constitution, and soon made a full recovery. Another attack occurred in August of the same year, Dr McCarthy came in again, and within a week Fred was back at work.

Meanwhile, Leonard Parsons's interest in his slatternly mistress was beginning to cool; perhaps he was becoming impatient because there was no prospect in sight of a more permanent arrangement. He left the cottage at the end of October and did not return. Charlotte was frantic. What could she do to bring him back?

On 11 December Fred was stricken once again with the symptoms of acute gastro-enteritis. He complained of a searing pain like a red-hot poker in his stomach. Dr McCarthy's remedies seemed to have little effect. Although her husband was so ill, Charlotte did not even have the common decency to stay and look after him but went off to tour the gypsy encampments in the area looking for Leonard Parsons. At one of these she encountered a severe shock – on asking for the whereabouts of her man, a woman named Priscilla Loveridge informed her that *she* was Leonard Parsons's common-law wife and had been for a good many years. She and her mother, a pipe-smoking old clothes-peg pedlar, screamed threats and abuse at Charlotte and chased her off the encampment. Charlotte's feelings on hearing these revelations can be more easily conjectured than described.

Charlotte returned home on 19 December, seething with rage. The next day Fred took a turn for the worse. A neighbour, Mrs Stone, and his employer's wife, Mrs Priddle, had been looking after him during Charlotte's absence, and these two good women, after giving Charlotte a sharp talking-to, called Dr McCarthy. By the time he arrived Fred's condition was rapidly deteriorating; he was almost comatose and unable to speak. Dr McCarthy ordered his immediate removal to the Yeatman Hospital, Sherborne, where he died the same afternoon.

Dr McCarthy was suspicious about the cause of death and refused to sign a death certificate. Instead, he went to the police and reported his feelings about the matter. An inquest was ordered on the 39-year-old labourer. Charlotte was ignorant as well as illiterate. 'What's an inquest?' she demanded. She was told that it was an investigation into the death of anyone who, it was thought, might have died of unnatural causes . . .

While police examined the Bryants' cottage, Charlotte and her five children were lodged in the Sturminster Newton workhouse (then called a 'Poor Law Institution'). The police called in the Yard after their forensic experts found traces of arsenic in the house, and the Yard's Detective Inspector Bell and Detective Sergeant Tapsell went over the house again with a fine-tooth comb. They swept cupboards, shelves, window-ledges and skirting-boards and, taking in all 146 samples of dust, dirt and refuse, they found that thirty-two of these samples contained traces of arsenic. Outside, in some rubbish, an empty weedkiller tin was found, which contained residues of arsenic.

Various items of circumstantial evidence were supplied by neighbours. A Mrs Ostler related that Charlotte had once said to her 'I hate Fred.' Mrs Ostler asked her why, in that case, she did not leave him, and the other woman's reply was that although she had a place she could go to herself, she would not be able to take all her children, and she did not want to leave them.

On another occasion Mrs Ostler was in the house helping to look after Fred during his last illness, and saw Charlotte giving her husband a cup of hot Oxo on the night before he died. She noticed that Charlotte took a good deal of care to wash out the cup afterwards – a thing she rarely bothered to do, preferring to leave crockery in the sink and wash it only when she had used all the others.

After Fred's death, Mrs Ostler was helping Charlotte clear up in the house, and she saw her friend take an empty weedkiller tin outside, saying, 'I must get rid of this. If they can't find anything, they can't put a rope around your neck.' Mrs Ostler thought the remark distinctly odd, but did not really give it much attention at the time.

The police discovered that an insurance agent, a Mr Tuck, had been approached by Mrs Bryant about a year previously, when she had said, 'I would like to insure my old man.' This was not followed up, but purely by chance Mr Tuck was in the vicinity on 20 December 1935, and decided to call on the off-chance. Fred Bryant was by then in a very bad way, and the insurance agent considered him to be a bad risk, so no policy was effected; instead, he drew up some small policies for the children. He arranged to call back on the 23rd for the premiums to be paid.

Mr Tuck was unaware that Fred Bryant had died since his last visit, and on the 23rd he found no one at home except the children, who did not know where their mother had gone or when she would return. Driving off, Mr Tuck encountered Charlotte Bryant and her friend Mrs Ostler walking home from a visit to a pub. He offered them a lift, during the course of which the women informed him of Fred's demise.

'Nobody can say I poisoned him,' Charlotte offered.

Mr Tuck was mystified by this remark. 'No – why should they?' he replied.

'Well, you never know,' she answered. 'Some people will say anything.'

Mr Tuck observed that, from her demeanour, no one would have imagined that she had just become a widow.

The police located Leonard Parsons, who readily admitted that he had had an affair with Charlotte Bryant for about 2½ years. He said that on one occasion Charlotte had told him that she would soon be a widow, and they would be able to marry. He had then told her that he already had a common-law wife, Priscilla Loveridge, with whom he had lived, on and off, at the gypsy encampment for about twelve years, and that she had borne him four children. This enraged Charlotte, who flounced out of the house in a huff.

On 10 February 1936 Superintendent Cherrett of the Sherborne police visited Mrs Bryant in the Sturminster Newton institution, where she was cautioned and formally charged with murdering her husband. Although no mention of poison had been made to her by the arresting officer, her reply was, to say the least, self-incriminating. 'I have never got any poison from anywhere . . . I don't see how they can say I poisoned my husband.'

She was taken to Exeter Prison, and her children remained in the institution. The NSPCC offered to find them homes, but they wished to stay together and there was no home available to take four lively youngsters aged twelve, ten, six and four, and a baby of fifteen months. The baby was almost certainly Leonard Parsons's child, but he neither denied nor admitted paternity.

The trial of Charlotte Bryant commenced on 27 May 1936 at the Dorset Assizes before Mr Justice MacKinnon. The Solicitor-General, Sir Terence O'Connor, KC, led for the Crown, and Charlotte Bryant was defended by Mr J. D. Casswell. The trial lasted four days.

Charlotte Bryant, who ate toffees as she sat in the dock, appeared to have little comprehension of the seriousness of her situation. During her evidence she insisted that she knew nothing about any poison, and denied having bought weedkiller, even when shown the empty container she had discarded, saying, 'I don't know how it got there.' She denied most of the prosecution's allegations including all the evidence given by Mrs Ostler. She maintained, too, that her relations with her husband had been good throughout their married life: 'Never a breath wrong with my husband in my life until Leonard Parsons came along.' In the witness-box, Parsons stolidly ignored her, even when she blew him kisses from the dock and was reprimanded by the judge for 'unseemly conduct in the courtroom.' Even her own counsel told her that she was taking everything far too lightly considering that she was on trial for her life. 'They can't hang me,' she said. 'I didn't poison my husband.' But they could, and did. On 30 May she was found guilty and sentenced to death.

The inevitable appeal followed, and on 29 June it was heard and dismissed. Mr Sidney Silverman, the abolitionist Labour MP for Nelson and Colne, asked the Home Secretary, Sir John Simon, whether he was aware that the Appeal Court judges had refused to admit certain additional evidence on the grounds that it could have been produced at the original trial where the defence had been conducted by junior counsel only, whereas the prosecution was heavily weighted with leading counsel and this could have unduly influenced a jury. The Home Secretary replied that, in his view, the defence had been well and adequately conducted.

Charlotte Bryant languished in Exeter Prison, refusing to see her children so as to avoid upsetting them any further. On 14 July, on the eve of her execution, she sent a last despairing telegram to the new King, Edward VIII, who was as yet uncrowned, but to no avail. Mrs van der Elst, a leading campaigner for the abolition of capital punishment, staged a demonstration outside the prison, and was fined five pounds for obstructing a policeman. Afterwards she said that she was going to set up a fund for the maintenance and education of Mrs Bryant's five children.

The law took its unrelenting course, and the unfortunate woman was hanged on 15 July 1936 at Exeter Prison. It was said that she went to her death bravely.

An inquest was held on her body, at which the jurors asked for permission to donate their fees to the fund for the Bryant children. The coroner replied that provision had already been made for them, and the jurymen then handed their fees to the prison governor with a request that they be given to the Discharged Prisoners' Aid Society.

It would be another thirteen years before a woman would be executed again in Britain.

12

The Fatal Blow

Bertie Manton (1942)

Council workmen had been sent to check the water levels of
the River Lea where it ran past the outskirts of Luton, in
Bedfordshire. The River Lea is not very big as rivers go, but
its water levels had a part to play in the scheme of things: a
new sewage-disposal project that the council had in blue-
print. The river was shallow and fringed with reed-beds,
but at this location it was not, unfortunately, a haven for
wildlife but a dumping-ground for refuse. Anything the
residents of the vicinity could not cram into their dustbins
they unceremoniously dumped in the River Lea.

Thus when, in the grey morning mist of Thursday, 19
November 1942, a number of old sacks, roped together,
wedged in the reeds and half-submerged, was seen by
several people hurrying to work at the nearby Vauxhall car
plant, no one took any particular notice. Just another load
of old rubbish, no doubt, was the unspoken thought that
might have crossed their minds fleetingly as they walked or
cycled, hoping that they were not late for clocking in.

Tom Steadman and his workmate, Len Phillips, clam-
bered down the bank with their water-level measuring
equipment. Tom spotted the largish parcel tied in sacking.
'Might as well take a dekko at this,' he said. 'Looks a bit
funny, doesn't it, Len?' And he tugged at the rope which
held the sacking together. A moment later he wished he
had left it alone.

'Christ!' he exploded. 'Get the police! It's a – a *body*!'

When police arrived, the body temperature had fallen to
that of the surroundings, and rigor mortis was fully established. The preliminary examination found the body to be
that of a woman of about thirty to thirty-five with dark hair

and brown eyes, five feet three inches tall. The body was naked, the feet had been tied together and the knees trussed up to the chest. She appeared to be pregnant, but this would be decided at the autopsy.

Police found tyre tracks twenty yards from the point where the body was found, but these were soon traced to a milkman's van that took the same route every morning, and the milkman was quickly eliminated. The police were not, in fact, convinced that the body had been transported to its last resting-place in a motor-car. The purpose of trussing the legs to the body, like a chicken, would most likely have been to enable the killer to make it more readily portable, and it could have been carried in a trolley, a trailer, a perambulator or a handcart. The sacks had been opened out and crudely roped together to wrap the cadaver, which, it was surmised, had been disrobed simply to facilitate wrapping the 'parcel'. Forensic examination revealed that one sack had contained soda, one sugar and two potatoes. All the sacks were common items with marks similar to others sold in the neighbourhood and could not be identified as having come from any particular source. One sack bore the letters MFD, but no firm – neither a sack manufacturer nor a producer or supplier of the goods which it had held – could be traced with these initials.

The autopsy, carried out by Home Office pathologist Professor Keith Simpson, revealed that the deceased's wedding ring had been removed as well as her false teeth. It was thought that this had been done to hinder identification. The fact that she had worn dentures was proved by the chafed condition of her gums, and it was also found that three roots had been left behind when teeth had been extracted; Simpson noted that this fact might prove helpful if her dentist could be located.

The woman had been in the twenty-second week of pregnancy, and had also previously borne at least one child, probably more. She had no distinguishing marks, such as moles, bunions and so on, except for a faded scar from an old appendectomy – but then so had a good many other people. Her fingerprints were not on record, so she had no criminal history. Her blood group was O – the commonest of the blood groups, found in more than half the white population. No foreign substances such as hairs were found under her nails or in the sacks. The body had not long been in the water, because the skin was still intact and there were no adipocerous changes; she had been immersed no longer than twenty-four hours.

Simpson, after these basic findings, now turned his attention to the important matter of the injuries on the body which could possibly point to the manner of the woman's death. An attempt had been made to strangle her; there was bruising on her neck, but this had not caused her death, and there were no 'voice-box' fractures. Bruises on her back and shoulders suggested that she had been flung against a wall or pinned to the floor; bruised elbows and knuckles proved that she had tried to struggle free from her attacker. Simpson found that a single violent blow, which had crushed the left side of her face, fractured both her jaws, loosened several skull bones and damaged the brain, had been the fatal blow. Other much less serious injuries on the other side of the face could have been caused by falling to the ground, and trauma to the scalp above the right ear could have been sustained by striking her head on the sharp edge of an item of furniture as she fell.

Meanwhile, while this painstaking forensic work was going on, the police were making equally painstaking inquiries. They managed to trace every one of the workmen who had been hot-footing it (or biking it) to work that morning and who had spotted the sacking parcel in the River Lea on their way to the Vauxhall plant; every one of them was adamant that the bundle had been there that morning of 19 November, but not on the previous day. This, of course, tied in nicely with the forensic findings that the body had been in the water for not more than twenty-four hours and possibly for only twelve. This latter was the most likely time-frame, because the council workmen, Tom Steadman and Len Phillips, who had found the body, stated positively that the time was 2.15 in the afternoon when they found it (Tom remembered looking at his watch at the time and telling the police officer who questioned him at the scene), and it was thought unlikely that the killer would have dumped the body in daylight, so it must be presumed that it had been left there some time after midnight, when no one would be about.

However, no further clues came to light to tie in nicely with any of the other findings. No woman in that age group had been reported missing in the area, and, as we have seen, a search for the source of the sacks had drawn a complete blank. In desperation, the police decided to issue a photograph and description to the media, in case someone might just recognize her. The victim's face, however, had been so badly shattered by the blunt instrument, that even with the most skilful repair work in the mortuary and retouching by the police photographer, the resulting photograph was a grotesque pastiche which bore little resemblance to a female face – it looked more like a wooden mask or dummy. Small wonder, then, that no one came forward. Even the woman's own children did not recognize her! Chief Inspector Chapman of the Yard remarked later that even her own mother would not have recognized her; but her mother, it turned out, was almost blind, and would probably not have recognized even a normal portrait of her daughter.

The photograph was flashed on cinema screens in the neighbourhood, and on one of those occasions the woman's daughter, aged seventeen, was attending the show, but she too failed to see any resemblance. The woman's two sons, aged fourteen and fifteen respectively, saw the photograph on a police poster displayed in a shop-window, and thought that it was vaguely reminiscent of their mother. On mentioning it to their father, who had told his children that their mother had gone to her mother's first and then on to her brother's in Grantham, he told the two boys that she had called at the house one day while they were at school to collect some clothes, on a date several days later than that on which the body had been found.

Chapman mounted the huge operation of sifting through no fewer than 404 missing women on police files, and all were either traced or eliminated from the inquiry. He was convinced, however, that the victim was a local woman, and that the killer was a local man; anyone else would have been very unlikely to know the spot on the reed-fringed banks of the River Lea where the body was found.

Because the left ring-finger of the victim showed the mark where a wedding band had been worn for some years and then removed, Chapman was convinced that she was a married woman, and that it was quite possible that she had been killed by her husband rather than a stranger. Murderous strangers do not usually kill their victims by hitting them in the face with a heavy blunt object, nor usually do they hang around long enough to truss up their victims and wrap them in sacking, even if they had such items with them at the time. No: this was a murder that had taken place indoors – probably in the woman's own home. The forensic evidence tended to bear this out: minor injuries were consistent with a fall against some hard wooden object such as the edge of a piece of furniture.

The public was invited to visit the mortuary and view the body in case anyone thought that he or she might know a person who had not been seen around or accounted for lately, and might be able to identify the victim. Thirty-nine people came to view the cadaver; obviously, there were those who had come simply out of morbid curiosity, but nine persons 'identified' the body as that of four other women!

Chapman's next move was the one which would eventually lead to a breakthrough in the case after three months of fruitless legwork. He decided to have all dry cleaners' and laundries' records searched for unclaimed or bloodstained clothing. Street refuse collections and council rubbish dumps were meticulously searched, and in addition no fewer than 250 lorry drivers were traced who had called at the Vauxhall car factory on or around the time of the murder, but after interviewing all of them they were eliminated. For the time being, Chapman had to admit defeat. This was indeed a baffling case.

House-to-house inquiries were organized throughout the entire area. An officer called at the house where the woman had lived, unaware of this fact, of course, and showed the police photograph to the woman's sons. Neither of them mentioned that they had thought the

photograph bore a faint resemblance to their mother when
they had seen it in the shop-window some weeks
previously, nor did they tell the officer that their mother
had left home at about the time of the discovery of the body.
The neighbours in the same street all failed to recognize the
photograph. The one or two who had inquired as to their
neighbour's whereabouts had been told by her husband
that she had gone to her mother's and subsequently to her
brother's in Grantham. He had given the same reply to an
inquiry from the Luton Food Office, and to a midwife who
had made a routine call to check on some details for the
antenatal clinic.

The hundreds, probably thousands, of pieces of rags and
old clothing that had been taken from rubbish dumps and
dustbins were still being microscopically examined in
police laboratories. One or two bore cleaners', dyers' and
laundries' identifying tags, or the remains of them, and it
was decided, almost as a last resort, to follow up all these.
Thus it was that a part of a dyer's tag – just a few numbers
on an inch of tape – came to Chapman's attention. It was
attached to part of an old black coat – a woman's coat – that
had been found in a dustbin. It was traced to a local branch
of Sketchley's, and in their books was the name of the
customer – a Mrs Rene Manton, who lived in Regent Street,
Luton. There was, of course, nothing at this stage to
connect it to the body which had been found in the River
Lea, and was now buried in a pauper's grave as a 'Jane
Doe'. But Chapman himself decided to pay the house a
visit. The door was opened by a little girl of eight. Chapman's heart missed a beat, for the child was the living image
of the dead woman.

Chapman showed his identity wallet. 'Is your mother at
home?' he asked.

'No, she's gone away. She's gone to live at Uncle Ray's in
Grantham. Did you want to see her?'

'Just making some inquiries,' the Chief Inspector
reassured her.

Chapman asked the little girl to show him a photograph
of her mother, which she did. That was it – it was the
woman they had fished from the River Lea. Of course

Chapman did not tell the child this but he asked to borrow the photograph, and also asked her for the address of the woman's mother. On visiting her, he found an infirm elderly lady, almost blind, who informed him that she had not seen her daughter for three months, and that as far as she knew her son in Grantham had not seen her either and she was certainly not staying with him. However, she said that she had received four letters from her daughter. She showed them to Chapman, who observed a number of spelling errors, including the word 'Hampstead' spelt without the 'p'. Chapman borrowed the letters and went back to the house in Regent Street, this time to ask the little girl where he could find her father.

Bertie Manton was a member of the National Fire Service, and Chapman found him at the local fire station where he was on duty. He and his wife had quarrelled, he told Chapman, and she had 'slung her hook', as he put it, saying she was going to her mother's and would probably arrange to stay with her brother afterwards. Asked what date this would have been, Manton replied that it was on 25 November (6 days *after* the body was found), and that he particularly remembered the date because it was on the last day of his leave. He recognized, of course, the photograph of his wife which Chapman had borrowed from his daughter, but not the police photograph. 'Good God, no!' he said. 'That's nothing like my wife! I wouldn't do anything like that. If she wants to leave me, good luck to her.' Chapman then showed him the four letters he had borrowed from Mrs Manton's mother, and he identified the handwriting as his wife's. Chapman then asked him to write a sentence containing the word 'Hampstead'. Manton wrote it in the same hand as that in which the four letters had been penned, omitting the 'p' in 'Hampstead', and making two other spelling errors which were contained in the letters. Chapman thanked him for his help and asked, almost casually, for the name of Mrs Manton's dentist. Manton was caught off guard: he told the Chief Inspector what he wanted to know.

The dentist at once recognized the photograph of the missing woman as she had looked in life, and he was able to show Chapman a record card giving the positions of three residual roots, which he had advised Mrs Manton to have extracted before being fitted for dentures, but she had refused. Their position corresponded exactly with those in the X-ray photographs of the dead woman's jaws, and the plaster casts which had been made.

At long last, Chapman exulted, his long and painstaking search had come to an end. He was not a man to give up easily: dogged persistence will achieve a great deal, even when almost insuperable difficulties block every avenue of progress. He went back to Bertie Manton and arrested him for the murder of his wife.

Manton broke down and confessed. 'I am sorry I told you so many lies,' he said. 'I killed her, but it was only because I lost my temper. I did not intend to. It's that fancy man of hers she kept going back to. She'd go away for several days and then come back again. We had a lot of rows about it, but this time I went too far. We quarrelled, and I killed her in the heat of passion. I lost my temper and bashed her with a wooden stool which I'd picked up because she jumped up from the table and threw a cup of tea at me. When I looked again, I saw she was dead. I didn't intend to kill her.'

At his trial for murder at Bedford Assizes, it was the forensic evidence that scotched Bertie Manton's claim that he had killed his wife unintentionally, thus qualifying the jury to bring in a verdict of manslaughter. It was Professor Simpson whose findings ruled this out; if the shattering head wound had been the only injury found, the outcome could have been very different.

Cross-examined by the prosecutor, Mr Richard O'Sullivan, KC, Manton was asked whether he had heard Professor Simpson tell the jury that there were marks upon the dead woman's neck consistent with pressure from a hand more than once. Manton replied that he remembered grabbing his wife by the throat and pushing her up against the wall. 'I may have grabbed her twice in my temper,' he conceded.

'You said nothing about that in your statement to the police,' the prosecutor went on relentlessly.

'No, sir,' Manton replied. 'I must have forgotten.'

Manton then described what he did after he had discovered that his wife was dead.

> I took off her rings and undressed her, and tied her up in the sacks. I then carried her down the cellar and left her there while I washed up the blood before the children came home from school. I told the children that she had gone to Gran's, and gave them their tea. The eldest daughter then went out to meet one of her friends, and I gave the other children money to go to the cinema. When it was completely dark I brought my wife up from the cellar, got my bike and laid her across the handlebars, and wheeled her down to Osborne Road. I laid her on the edge of the river bank and she rolled into the river. Then I rode home and got the children's supper ready. They never suspected anything.

The next day he burned the bloodstained clothing in the copper together with her false teeth. He thought that he ought to get rid of his wife's coat, for it would be considered odd if she had left home in mid-November without it and she did not have another one. He cut it into pieces and distributed them in various dustbins in the area after dark.

When the police searched the house, forensic technicians found traces of Group O blood – Rene Manton's group – in various parts of the living-room. They also found a writing-pad and envelopes identical to those which had been used for the writing of the four letters to the dead woman's mother. Finally, after a search of some dusty bottles and jars in the pantry, fingerprint experts found a left thumb-print on an empty pickle jar which was identical to the dead woman's left thumbprint. The dust of three months had made the fingerprint men's task easier. The heavy oak stool with which Rene Manton had been done to death was not found, and the prisoner was asked what had happened to it. He replied that he had told his eldest son to chop it up for firewood.

On his conviction for murder, Bertie Manton was sentenced to death, but a petition for mercy bearing 30,000 signatures was submitted to the Home Office, and he was reprieved. His health, which had never been robust, was already in decline, and three years after his conviction he died in prison.

13

The Chalkpit Murder

Thomas Ley and Lawrence Smith (1946)

For a jealous man to murder a woman, or his rival in love, is reprehensible enough, but for a man to plot such a murder and pay two men to carry out the dirty work on his behalf, is infinitely worse. Especially when the murdered man is a perfectly innocent individual who had no possible claim upon the attentions of the woman with whom he was accused of having a liaison: in fact the only time he ever met her was when passing her once on the stairs when she was staying for a few days in the same house! And the crime which is the subject of this chapter is all the more bizarre because the jealous man, whose mistress the woman concerned had been for twenty-five years, had become impotent about ten years before the crime and their sexual relationship had ended!

Near Woldingham, in Surrey, a chalkpit was cut into the barren hillside, and at the bottom a narrow trench had been dug to facilitate drainage at the time the pit had been worked, since the men could not quarry the chalk if the pit filled with water every time it rained. Now, at the time our story opens, the chalkpit was long disused, and the area was as desolate a place as any that could be found in the county. Few people walked that way; even couples rarely used it as a lovers' lane, for it would have been difficult to park a car there.

One man, however, decided to walk his dog in the vicinity of the pit on the evening of 30 November 1946. The man, Walter Coombs, let his black-and-white crossbred collie off the lead, and the dog ran forward, enjoying the unaccustomed freedom. Usually, owing to the number of sheep farmed in the area, he kept the dog on a leash when he walked him.

Coombs stopped by an ash tree several yards from the chalkpit to shelter from the wind while he lit his pipe. Puffing contentedly, he called the dog, but the animal ignored his whistles and ran backwards and forwards along the edge of the top of the chalkpit, whining and barking. Coombs decided to go and investigate the cause of his dog's excitement. What he saw made him take off at speed, with the dog in tow, to look for a policeman.

Dr Eric Gardner, called to the scene by police officers working by lamplight, for it was by then already dark, estimated that the body which Coombs had seen was that of a man aged about thirty-five, who had been dead about forty-eight hours. His face was suffused from asphyxiation, and there was a noose around his neck. His body, which was fully clothed, lay on its side in the trench at the bottom of the pit, which was six feet long and just wide enough – it could have been dug for the purpose of a hasty burial, but this was not the case: the trench had been excavated at least eight years earlier. Whoever had left the body there would seem to have fortuitously discovered just the right location for the purpose, but no attempt had been made to cover the body. Perhaps this has been the intention, the person or persons who had left the body being frightened off by something, or someone.

The ground in and around the trench was a sea of mud, so much so that the shoes of the police officers and medical personnel were soon plastered ankle-deep. Rain had fallen in recent days, not enough to flood the pit but sufficient to render the investigators' movements very difficult. However, there was no mud at all on the dead man's shoes – even the soles were clean. This made it quite clear that he had been carried to the makeshift grave, and had certainly never walked there, which, again, would imply that he had been killed elsewhere.

It was noted that a length of soft green cloth was entwined with the noose, which was so loose that it could easily be slipped over his head, and that his braces, were attached to the trouser buttons only at the back. Was this a masochistic hanging that had gone wrong? An autopsy would point the way to a clearer picture of how the man had met his end.

The autopsy was performed by Dr Gardner at the Oxted mortuary. Evidence of asphyxia was undeniable: suffusion of the head and neck, many small *petechiae* (tiny haemorrhages in the whites of the eyes from the bursting of minute blood-vessels), and deep cyanotic congestion of all the internal organs, particularly in the lungs, as well as haemorrhages of blood-vessels in the heart, brain and the small intestine.

A rope burn encircled the neck, and if this had been horizontal it would have implied strangling with a garotte. But the mark was not horizontal; it was lowest and deepest on the right side, and considerably higher on the left, rising to an inverted V-shaped point below the ear. This was a typical suspension-point: a classic textbook case of hanging. Or was it?

Dr Gardner did not think that it was suicide. It certainly looked as though the rope had broken or come loose and the man had fallen to the ground; but even if this had been the case it could not have taken place at this spot, because the nearest tree from which anyone could hang himself was several yards away from the pit. Nor could he have fallen into the trench without his shoes having become muddied, as well as his clothing, which was clean.

There were a few trivial abrasions on the head, including a bruise to the forehead which was not visible on the surface; there was another small bruise on the left hip joint, and two rib fractures on the right side with associated bruising. These bruises and injuries were too slight to have been the result of a struggle, and his hands bore no marks. His clothing was not torn or cut.

Another possibility that could not be ruled out in these early stages was that he had hanged himself from one of the trees in the vicinity and been found dead by a chance passer-by, who had cut down the body and hastily dumped it in the trench before leaving the scene, so as not to become involved. However, two facts seemed to eliminate that theory: the rope around the man's neck had not been cut, and a search of the trees revealed no evidence of any branches at the appropriate height from the ground having been used in such a manner. There would have to have been rope strands, fibres from the green cloth and marks where the noose had cut into the bark.

In the mean time, an identity card – still carried in 1946 although the war had ended – was found in the dead man's pocket, so he was at least quickly identified and did not cause the police additional problems by being a 'John Doe'. The dead man was John McMain Mudie, a 35-year-old barman who had been working in the Reigate Hill Hotel, about twelve miles from where his body was found. He had last been seen alive at about 5 p.m. on the previous Thursday, leaving the hotel for his half-day. Dr Gardner's estimate of the time of death was thus proved to be accurate within an hour or two. Mudie had been working at the hotel for several months; his employers stated that he was quiet and unassuming, and certainly not the kind of person to commit suicide. A search of his room provided no clues in the form of books or magazines catering to masochistic or other perversions, and this angle was eliminated. His previous landlady was traced, and she said that Mudie was a nice quiet lodger who gave no trouble. He had been lodging at her house for only six weeks when he was offered the barman's job at the Reigate Hill Hotel, which included a room. She was sorry to see him go, she added.

In Mudie's room at the hotel, police found no clues to his unexplained death, but they did find something which at first sight appeared to have no connection with the mystery. It was a letter addressed to him at his former lodgings in Wimbledon, asking him to pass on some cheques to the director of a property company, who happened to be staying in the same house, in the flat of a friend, this flat consisting of all the rooms on the second floor. Apparently Mudie had been in no hurry to return the cheques, for a further letter was found, this time addressed to him at the Reigate Hill Hotel, asking him to attend to the matter forthwith. What never seemed to be made clear was what interest Mudie had in cheques made out to a property company; he had no real-estate interest, or even a bank account.

Detective Sergeant Frederick Shoobridge went to Wimbledon and asked Mrs Evans, Mudie's former landlady, what she knew, if anything, about the property company mentioned in the letters. Mrs Evans told the detective that the director of the company, a Mrs Byron Brook, had stayed in the house for about ten days, in the flat of a woman friend who occupied the second floor. She knew nothing of any letters, and volunteered the information that she had introduced Mrs Brook and John Mudie during a chance meeting as they had passed each other on the stairs, and that as far as she knew that was the only time that the two had met one another.

*   *   *

The police issued a statement to the Press that 'a dead body' had been found in the chalkpit, giving no more information about it, and appealing for the public to come forward. Had anyone seen or heard anything suspicious in that area on the date in question? Two gardeners who had been walking home from work on the Wednesday prior to the finding of the body reported that they had seen a man behaving in a suspicious manner. The man had been standing on the edge of the chalkpit for several minutes, not walking about but merely looking down into the pit. Suddenly he spotted them, at which he turned on his heel and ran very fast to the path skirting the edge of the trees, jumped into a parked car, revved up and reversed out at speed. The gardeners did not have a clear view of the man's face, but thought that the car was either a Ford or an Austin, a small dark-coloured saloon, eight or ten horsepower, and both men said that three consecutive figures in the registration number were 101, but they could not recall the letters.

The next stage of the investigation was a visit by Detective Sergeant Shoobridge to the firm of solicitors who had sent the two letters to Mudie. They were hoping that they might be able to throw some light on what seemed to be a most baffling enigma. The solicitors told Shoobridge that they had been instructed by the chairman of the property company, a Mr Thomas Ley, who lived in Beaufort Gardens, Kensington. Shoobridge went to interview him.

Ley, a huge fat man, sixty-six years of age, invited Shoobridge in and breezily told him that 'it was all a misunderstanding'. For some reason, he explained, he had thought, as it turned out mistakenly, that Mudie was a friend of Mrs Brook. Because Mrs Brook had left her friend's flat in Wimbledon by the time the cheques had arrived for her, and he knew that Mudie still lived in the house, he assumed that he (Mudie) would be able to pass the cheques on to her, because he was under the impression that they were friends. It all sounded very complicated to Shoobridge, who asked Ley for the name of the person who had drawn the cheques, but Ley declined to reveal this, saying that the matter was private.

Shoobridge decided to call on the firm of property developers at their offices, and eventually found the filed carbon copy of the letter which had been sent to Mudie enclosing the cheques. One sentence read: 'Mrs Byron Brook had directed us to send her the cheques, care of yourself, so that you may hand them to her in person.'

At this point Detective Superintendent Roberts, chief of the Surrey County CID, took over the case from Shoobridge. He decided to investigate Thomas Ley as discreetly as possible, for he felt sure that there was something in this mystery that needed looking into and that there was more than met the eye behind the machinations of Ley and Mrs Brook, even if Mudie had been merely an unwitting pawn. It seemed that Ley was not only a qualified solicitor in his own right, but was a former Minister of Justice in New South Wales, Australia. He had returned to England in 1930, followed shortly afterwards by Mrs Brook who, it turned out, had been his mistress for the past twenty-five years. She was the same age as Ley, and although for the past ten years their sexual relationship had been non-existent, owing to his impotence, his love for her was, however, undiminished; she still lived with him, but more in the role of housekeeper and companion. Ley's jealousy of her increased to the point of obsession, and there were

frequent rows about other men – mostly very young men –
in whom Mrs Brook was not the slightest bit interested. She
had reached the age of sixty-six, and certainly did not look
any younger, when Ley started accusing her, quite absurd-
ly, of having sexual intercourse with no fewer than three
young men, all tenants of the house in Wimbledon. One of
them was her own son-in-law; another was the unfortunate
John McMain Mudie: 'I only met him once, and that was
just in passing him on the stairs when Mrs Evans introduced us,' she said. Mrs Brook, when interviewed, was not
in the least reticent about revealing all these personal
details to the police.

Detective Superintendent Roberts now felt that the death
of Mudie was nothing to do with any business deals,
cheques or anything of that nature, but that it might have
had a good deal to do with Ley's unfounded jealousy. The
passion of a virile man is one thing, but the frustrated
passion of an impotent man is something else again, and it
can well be deadly . . .

Roberts decided to call in the aid of Scotland Yard, and
Detective Chief Inspector Arthur Philpott was sent to take
charge of the case. Philpott was a tough and uncompromis-
ing policeman who was not one to be fazed by a former
Minister of Justice, or to quibble with the pathologist who
had said that the medical evidence would not support a
murder charge. Eric Gardner conceded that Mudie might
have been 'roughed up', as he put it, and also that he had
never had a case of a suicide hanging himself with a noose
tied in a single half-hitch, which would produce a slow and
agonizing death from asphyxiation. Professor Keith Simpson, the Home Office forensic pathologist, who had had
much more experience in such matters than Dr Gardner,
ventured to disagree on this latter point. Such cases did
occur, he said, albeit infrequently. He did not rule out
murder, but considered that it would have been virtually
impossible for an elderly and obese man like Ley to have
killed a young, strong and fit man like Mudie. He could
certainly not have carried a body to that chalkpit. If it had
indeed been murder, was it possible that Ley could have
hired someone else to do the job?

It is very difficult to hire a 'hit-man' in this country, and even more difficult if the killer hired a small-time thug who did not realize that murder was intended rather than merely beating up the victim. If Ley had in fact hired someone to lure Mudie to his death, but without knowing that he was to be killed, such a man, on learning that the victim was dead, would be very scared when he realized that he had been, albeit unwittingly, an accessory to murder. Philpott's ruminations on this theory led him to give the Press a little more information. The name of the dead man, together with his photograph, might just trigger developments . . .

He was right in this surmise, but the developments were quite different from those he had anticipated. Within a few hours of the story appearing in the newspapers, an ex-boxer named John William Buckingham – unable to live with his conscience – went to Scotland Yard and told a senior officer that Ley had paid him £200 to kidnap Mudie, who (Ley said) had been paying unwelcome attentions to his lady-friend. He said that the intention was to force Mudie to sign a confession and leave the country. A woman friend of Buckingham's was employed to decoy Mudie to Ley's Kensington house, where Buckingham and an accomplice named Lawrence Smith were waiting for him. They pushed him into a front room and the woman decoy was told to make herself scarce. 'There was no fight or struggle,' Buckingham said. 'We just shut the door on him. Ley paid me the money and I left as fast as I could with Smith.'

The police soon traced Smith, a foreman joiner whom Ley knew from his having done some carpentry work in his house. He confirmed part of his accomplice's story, but said that when Mudie entered the house Buckingham was waiting for him, holding a rug, while Smith held a clothes-line. Smith went on:

We kidnapped him by throwing the rug over his head, and my job was to tie the clothes-line round his arms, legs and body so that he could not escape, but leaving the rug loose enough so that he could breathe, but not shout or anything like that . . .

John [Buckingham] 'jumped' him along the hall from the room
and into another smaller room where we were going to keep
him prisoner until he had signed the confession, and after that
we were going to put him in a car and see him to the airport . . .
When we got to this other room, he tripped, and John fell on
top of him . . . John picked him up and sat him in a swivel chair
where Ley had told us to put him. John then asked me to look
for a gag. I found a french polisher's rag to use. John pulled the
rug off Mudie's head and I tied the gag round his mouth, just
so he couldn't shout – he could breathe OK.

Smith finally said that Buckingham left, and that he himself
left about ten minutes later, having also been paid £200 by
Ley for his trouble. He said he knew nothing whatever of
Mudie's death, but he identified the length of green cloth
intertwined with the noose as the french polisher's rag.

Philpott confronted Buckingham with Smith's statement. The ex-boxer agreed that he had thrown a rug over
Mudie's head while Smith tied him up, and that he had
'jumped' him along the passage, but he denied that Mudie
had tripped and fallen or that a gag had been used. Philpott
then went to see Ley and invited him to come to the Yard to
make a statement. Ley sent for his solicitor and denied the
whole story, saying he knew nothing of Mudie's death and
that the two men, both of whom he knew, had made the
whole thing up. It was preposterous, he said. Obviously
they had some grudge against him and wanted to discredit
him.

Philpott still had insufficient evidence to arrest the three
men. He arranged a meeting with Dr Gardner and Professor Simpson to clarify some of the finer points of the
forensic evidence. Gardner said that the rug over the head
explained the absence of a surface bruise sustained by a
bang on the forehead when he tripped and fell. Buckingham's falling on top of him could have caused the internal
haemorrhages. There was no object in the room from which
he could have been hanged. But it was still not enough to
warrant bringing his kidnappers in on a murder charge.
The three suspects still walked free.

Delving into the immediate background of the suspects,
Philpott discovered that Smith had hired a car, a dark-

coloured Ford, eight horsepower, with the registration number FGP 101. Philpott then put Smith on an identity parade and called the two gardeners who had seen the man standing at the edge of the chalkpit. One of them picked Smith out immediately; the other picked out a different man.

On this additional evidence the case was still rather weak, and the Director of Public Prosecutions allowed Buckingham to be a prosecution witness with a guarantee of immunity. This, it was considered, would bring the case to trial and, it was hoped, decide where the truth of these matters lay.

The Lord Chief Justice himself (Lord Goddard) presided over the trial; the prosecution was led by Mr Anthony Hawke and Mr Henry Elam, and Smith was defended by Mr Derek Curtis-Bennett and Mr Malcolm Morris. Ley, of course, could afford to instruct two of the most famous counsel of the day, Sir Walter Monckton and Mr Gerald Howard.

The main points of the trial were the various aspects of the medical evidence, some of which was controversial. Dr Gardner and Professor Simpson both gave detailed evidence, often in conflicting terms: Gardner inclined more to the view that Mudie had been beaten up and that this had caused the various injuries; whereas Simpson's view was that these traumas had been caused by a fall, followed by one of his assailants' falling on top of him.

But by far the most important part of the forensic evidence was the description of the appearance of the dead man's neck. It was more in keeping with a hanging than a strangulation, and this theory was amply borne out by the type of mark found on the neck. But there was no evidence at all that the victim had been suspended from a high object. There was nothing in either the first or the second room in which Mudie had been kept after the kidnapping, and the hat-pegs in the hall were at the wrong height for the purpose. The only possible solution to the enigma was the speculative theory that one or both of the kidnappers had stood behind Mudie as he sat, trussed with the clothes-line and gagged with the oily polisher's rag, and pulled the noose upwards, tightening it automatically as he did so. This proved to be the most contentious issue in the evidence.

After a great deal of long-drawn-out argument between cross-examining counsel, Dr Gardner and Professor Simpson about the origin of the various bruises and other injuries on the head and body, they came to the crux of the matter: the trauma to the neck. 'Anyone could have killed Mudie by lifting the noose and holding it up for two or three minutes,' Simpson said. When asked by counsel if he had anyone in mind, Simpson adroitly replied that it was not his job to name suspects, but only to present the medical evidence, as he saw it, as clearly as possible.

Sir Walter Monckton's cross-examination of Dr Gardner was relentless. Turning to the photographs of the rope burns on Mudie's neck, he left Gardner in no doubt of his intentions: 'It is right, is it not, that there is an indication that he was pulled up at some stage?'

'There was an indication of some tension upwards.'

'Did you take the view,' continued the prosecutor, 'that the rope marks indicated that the deceased was suspended by it?'

'I said that there was some degree of suspension.'

'Did you say in your original report that there was no doubt that the deceased was suspended by the rope?'

Gardner was clearly disconcerted by the direction that these questions were taking. 'I cannot remember,' he said.

'I would be extremely grateful if you would look into your notes.'

'You are going back a long time, sir, you know,' the doctor replied as he leafed through his sheaf of papers, finally agreeing that he had said there had been some form of suspension. 'But,' he added firmly, 'there had been no drop.'

The judge here came to the rescue. 'You did not think he had been hanged, in the ordinary sense of the word?'

'No, my lord, I did not.'

Next it was Simpson's turn to be cross-examined. 'There was evidence only of suspension and tightening,' he replied to questioning. 'There was nothing to indicate whether death was due to an accident, suicide, or murder.'

Sir Anthony Hawke, in cross-examining Simpson, did not seriously dispute this statement, but he made a telling point. 'Did Mudie die as a result of asphyxia caused by having a rope tied tightly round his neck?'

'Tied *and lifted*,' Simpson replied.

'You want to add "lifted"?'

'Yes,' the Professor replied. 'It was the lifting that did it.'

Next to be brought into evidence, appropriately at this point, were the police photographic enlargements of Mudie's neck. On developing and printing, one of these showed a straight line, invisible to the naked eye, which formed a base to the angle of suspension beneath the left ear. This proved conclusively, the experts averred, that the noose had been tightened before being lifted. The rope had first been drawn tightly in a horizontal position; then it had been lifted and held thus for at least two or three minutes. This would cause death by asphyxiation. It was, they insisted, scarcely likely that a man would, or even could, strangle or hang himself in such a manner. Thus the facts of the case pointed to murder – a murder performed in such a way as to make it look like suicide by hanging. But once again the killer, or killers, had not reckoned with the skill of the forensic pathologists . . .

With a prior reconnoitring of the grave-site, the method of murder chosen must have been premeditated too; this was borne out by the elaborate 'kidnap' plot. Ley was proved to have paid each of his two stooges £200 for his role in the slaying, and it is more than likely that the two killers did not hatch the murder plot between themselves only, but that Ley was not only the instigator but also acted in what could be termed an advisory capacity. To quote Smith's own statement: 'Ley had told us to put him [Mudie] in the swivel chair.' That would imply that Ley had told the two men which room to take Mudie into; and surely it was not just fortuitous that a rug light enough and small enough to throw easily over the victim's head just 'happened' to lie on the floor of that room at the time.

Ley was sentenced to death, but on 5 May 1947 he was

reprieved and sent to Broadmoor, which in those days was still called Broadmoor Criminal Lunatic Asylum. Smith was also sentenced to death and reprieved, his sentence being commuted to penal servitude for life.

On 24 July 1947, barely eleven weeks after his committal, Ley died of a brain haemorrhage. Whatever the reasons for his reprieve – and the Home Secretary never divulges his reasons – it is tempting to speculate that the prospect of having to hang Ley would have given Pierrepoint quite a headache. Ley weighed twenty-two stone.

14

Dear John . . .

Leslie George Stone (1936)

Four years is a long time by anyone's standards, and
especially so to a healthy and attractive young girl of
twenty-three, who had been unofficially engaged to a
builder's labourer a year older than herself – unofficially
because he had not given her a ring, but their respective
families and friends had all assumed that one day they
would marry. They seemed ideally suited; it had been a
boy-and-girl sweetheart kind of friendship, and they had
known each other for about seven years. They didn't live
next door, but in neighbouring communities: she with her
widowed mother, sister and brother in the Bedfordshire
town of Leighton Buzzard, he in a village a mile away called
Heath and Reach.

The girl, Ruby Keen, worked in a factory in the nearby
town of Dunstable. She was an assiduous worker, a good
timekeeper and had a good reputation among her work-
mates and superiors. When she was free she liked to have a
good time, enjoying the social whirl, attending dances and
indulging in the mildest of mild flirtations. She was not
promiscuous, but enjoyed the attentions of boys who
escorted her to dances and socials, or to the pub for a quiet
drink. Her steady sweetheart was not much of a dance fan –
he was quiet and preferred radio and reading.

In 1932 the erstwhile builder's labourer decided that he
had had enough of hod-carrying and concrete-mixing, and
decided to join the Army and see the world. He was
accepted into the Royal Artillery and was soon posted to
Hong Kong, which was not the world, but it was a start.
Ruby wrote to him regularly for the first year or so, but
after that her letters became less frequent, and finally so

infrequent that her soldier boyfriend wrote to ask her for an explanation. Had she found someone else?

Ruby wrote him what is called a 'Dear John' – a letter to tell him that their 'understanding' was at an end. She explained that as he would be in Hong Kong for a total of four years, it was really too long for him to keep her on a string. She was almost half-way to thirty already, and did not want to end up on the shelf. And, she pointed out as diplomatically as she could, a serving private soldier who would be overseas for four years was not really the kind of husband she wanted, much less a father for her children – they would hardly ever see each other! What kind of family was that?

The recipient of the 'Dear John' wasn't named John, but Leslie George Stone, and he took the news rather badly. However, he was not one to make a song and dance about it and broadcast his wounded feelings to his mates, but kept to himself the mortification and injured pride that he undoubtedly felt. He threw himself into his duties and decided to become a soldier the Army could be proud of.

Meanwhile, back in Leighton Buzzard, Ruby Keen soon forgot about the young man whose feelings for her were obviously stronger than vice-versa. Before long she was dancing and flirting again with little, if any, thought for the lovelorn Leslie. Out of sight, out of mind, as they say. Inevitably, among the personable and eligible young fellows she was bound to meet in the social whirl, she met one who obviously meant more to her than some nebulous young chap in far-off Hong Kong. He was a policeman with the Bedfordshire Constabulary, the same age as herself, and in 1936 they became engaged – officially this time, with the giving of a solitaire diamond ring. His policeman's pay would not run to it, so his father loaned him the money. From this it would seem obvious that not only was the young couple serious but also the parents were happy with the engagement.

Quite soon after the engagement had been announced, in December 1936, Leslie Stone was discharged from the Army on medical grounds, but with an exemplary serving record. He returned home and began to look for a job.

It was not until two months later that he was in Leighton Buzzard one day and spotted Ruby Keen in the street, walking with a policeman. He had already heard rumours that she was engaged to be married to a local beat copper. Leslie did not approach the couple, but stood staring at them as though in a daze. They did not appear to have seen him as he stood in the shadows.

He decided to keep a look-out for her when she was alone – perhaps doing the Saturday shopping for her mother. Eventually he saw her on her way to church, on Sunday, 4 April. After the service he contrived to be walking outside the church when she came out.

'Hello,' he said. 'Long time no see! How about a drink?' The Golden Bell pub was nearby.

In the pub, he said that they ought to have a night out on the town together for old times' sake.

'Don't mind if I do,' she unwisely agreed, 'some time when I see you around.' She would not commit herself to a definite date.

A week later Ruby attended a church service with a girlfriend, and after leaving the other girl to go home Ruby dropped into the Golden Bell at about 7 p.m. Leslie Stone, having seen her go to the church, had more or less antici-pated that she might nip into the pub for a quick drink before going home – more on the off-chance of seeing some of her friends than for the sake of the drink, for Ruby was a very sociable girl. Leslie had put on his new navy-blue serge suit, which he had not worn before. He strode purposefully over to Ruby and bought a glass of port for her and a pint of mild for himself. He had two more pints before they moved on to the Cross Keys, and finally to the Stag Hotel. As they sat in a corner of the saloon bar, some other customers overheard their conversation: Leslie was trying to persuade Ruby to give up her policeman fiancé and marry him.

'After all,' he was heard to say, 'you've known me the best part of ten years – how long have you known this other chap – three years at the very outside!'

Her reply to this sally had been, according to one witness: 'What can you offer me? You're unemployed; he has a steady job. He's given me an engagement ring; you never did. And four years was a long time for you to be away. What did you think I would do – become a nun?'

After ordering two more pints of mild for himself and two more glasses of port for his companion, Leslie and Ruby were seen to leave the Stag Hotel just before closing-time at ten o'clock. They were next seen walking past Ruby's home in Plantation Lane and entering the Firs, a pine-shaded 'lovers' lane' about 300 yards from the girl's home. A married couple who took a short cut home along this lane reported seeing Ruby, whom they knew, in the arms of a policeman. Asked why they thought the man was a policeman, they said that he was wearing 'a dark navy-blue uniform'. Anyway, they pointed out, they knew that Ruby was engaged to a policeman!

                    *   *   *

A railwayman named Cox was on his way to work at seven o'clock the next morning when he had the shock of his life. Crossing the lane in order to reach the railway lines which ran alongside the nearby embankment, he came upon the almost naked body of a young girl, sprawled on its face in the dew. No attempt had been made to conceal the body. Police called to the scene found that she had been strangled with her own black silk scarf. Most of her clothing had been torn off in a frenzy and scattered about, but the dead girl was still incongruously wearing her gloves. Robbery was ruled out; her handbag was untouched. It appeared that she had been resisting an attempted rape, although she had not been sexually assaulted. The sandy soil, greatly disturbed, bore mute witness to her desperate struggle, and the imprints of a man's knees showed that her assailant had knelt beside the body. Inquiries at nearby cottages, almost all of whose occupants kept dogs, drew a blank; not a single dog had barked, so the attack must have been a swift and noiseless one.

On the afternoon of 12 April Leslie Stone called at a friend's house and asked his friend's wife to telephone Leighton Buzzard police station and tell them that he

wanted to make a statement, because he had been out with
Ruby the previous evening, and that he wanted to set the
record straight and clear himself of any involvement in her
death. He told his friend's wife that he had only just read of
Ruby's death in the local paper, after coming home for
lunch having been out looking for work. The woman later
said that Leslie appeared very agitated: he had obviously
had a great shock. She did get in touch with the police in a
roundabout way: her husband had a friend who was a
policeman, and she told him. But the police at the town's
headquarters seemed little interested in Leslie Stone. They
were more interested in the evidence of the couple who had
been in the Firs, who had averred that they saw Ruby with a
policeman. Could one of their officers have been involved?

They decided that this possibility was too fraught to
justify their dealing with the case themselves, and they
hastened to call in Scotland Yard, which sent Chief Inspector Barker to look into the matter. First of all, Barker went to
question the young bobby who had been Ruby's fiancé and
who, it turned out, had planned to marry her in August of
that year. He had a cast-iron alibi: he had been on duty that
evening in the village of Hockliffe – three miles from
Leighton Buzzard – after seeing Ruby in the afternoon.

Footprints at the scene had been trampled during the
fatal struggle and were too confused to be of any use, but
plaster casts were made of the knee-prints. When these
were subjected to forensic examination by Sir Bernard
Spilsbury, a clear impression of the trouser-crease and the
weave of the material was found. It was decided to pull in
for questioning again all the possible suspects in the case –
Ruby's fiancé, several of her male acquaintances and
friends, and Leslie Stone. They were all asked to produce
for microscopical examination in the forensic laboratory the
trousers they had worn on the night of 11 April.

All the other men's trousers passed the most rigorous
testing, but the trousers to Leslie Stone's new navy-blue
suit – which, it seemed, had looked just like a policeman's
uniform to the couple in the lane – were made of material
identical in weave to the pattern shown in the plaster casts
of the knee-prints. Furthermore, the knees of the trousers

themselves had been brushed so hard that the nap of the material had been worn away, even though the suit was new and had been worn that night for the first time. Sir Bernard Spilsbury also found granules of sandy soil not only in the material at the knees but also on other parts of the trousers. These were identical to the soil particles present at the scene of the crime. Since Leslie Stone admitted that he had not worn the suit before that night, he could not claim to have got sandy soil on to his trousers on a previous occasion.

An incriminating item was a single cream-coloured silk fibre found embedded in the lining of Leslie Stone's jacket. It matched exactly the cream silk slip which Ruby had been wearing under her dress on the night she met her death.

Leslie Stone was arrested and charged with the murder of Ruby Keen on 24 April 1937, and the trial was set for 28 June at the Old Bailey before the then Lord Chief Justice, Lord Hewart. Mr Richard O'Sullivan, KC, prosecuted, assisted by Mr Christmas Humphreys. Stone was defended by Mr Maurice Healy, KC.

Evidence for both the prosecution and the defence was somewhat scanty and mainly circumstantial. The judge severely took to task the evidence of the couple in the lane. Quite apart from the fact that it was dark at the time, and they could not have been certain that the man they saw was wearing a policeman's uniform, their evidence was coloured by the assumption from prior knowledge that Ruby had been engaged to a policeman. It was a classic example of evidence being clouded by pre-knowledge.

Although initially Stone had pleaded not guilty to the charge, on the second day of the trial he suddenly and dramatically changed his story as he stood in the witness-box. He now admitted that he and Ruby had quarrelled over her forthcoming marriage, and that she had slapped his face when he made a derogatory remark about her fiancé. He flew into a rage and grabbed her by the throat. She then swung her handbag at him, catching him on the side of the head, and he pushed her roughly, whereupon she struck him with the other hand and he pulled on the scarf which she was wearing round her neck and choked her in his fury. 'I think I knotted it after that,' he went on, 'and she started to fall . . . I grabbed her clothes to stop her from falling and they ripped in the struggle. Most of them were all torn off as she fell'. Counsel at this point voiced the opinion that a body falling to the ground would not have all its clothes ripped off unless somebody had ripped them.

Undeterred, Stone continued with his testimony. 'I knelt on the ground beside her, but she was only stunned, not dead. I did not interfere with her. I walked away, feeling sure that she would come to, get up and go home. I then went home and brushed my clothes . . .'

A less believable story would have been hard to use as a defence, and the jury did not believe it for one moment. After only twenty-five minutes they came back with a unanimous verdict of guilty, and Stone was sentenced to death.

Stone appealed against the verdict on the grounds that the jury had been misdirected by the judge. It was on record that when the jury had questioned him on a point of law, his reply had been too unequivocal to be considered as being unbiased. They had asked him whether a man is guilty of murder if he kills a girl as a result of an intention to commit rape, even though he had no conscious intention of killing her, and the judge had replied, 'Yes, undoubtedly'. The Appeal Court, however, did not question the Lord Chief Justice's impartiality on this point, ruling that both the question and the answer were right and proper in law. They dismissed the appeal.

Friday the 13th was an unlucky day for Leslie Stone, for in August, on that date, he was hanged in Pentonville.

15

The Wigwam Girl

August Sangret (1942)

Between Godalming and the Hog's Back in the Surrey hills lies Hankley Common, a heathland typical of several such areas in the region. In spring the common is aflame with gorse and broom, while slender silver birches burst into leaf. In summer the heather is growing apace, but not until autumn does its purple blossom cover the gentle slopes with a blaze of glory. Bracken which in spring coils from the ground between the sparse pines in lush green fiddle-heads and in summer can stand as tall as a man, now, as the year draws to a close in the mellow autumn sunlight, dons hues of russet and bronze before returning to the earth in death, leaving in many places bare mounds of soil.

It was just such a mound of earth that attracted the attention of two Marines engaged on exercises on the common on 7 October 1942. William Moore and his companion Geoffrey Cooke were crawling, belly to ground, in a mock battle, taking cover among the scrub, when Moore spotted what looked to him like a human arm protruding from a mound of earth.

'Hey, Geoff!' he called. 'Come and look at this!' Cooke hurried over to where his fellow soldier lay prone, staring at the unexpected sight.

'Looks like somebody has been buried here,' he said. 'We'd better report this to the CO.'

'He'll simply *love* you if you try to locate him during an exercise!' Moore warned. 'We'll find the NCO and *he'll* call in the cops.' Moore straightened up. 'It's a woman's arm,' he observed. 'Tell you what. You stay here and keep guard while I go and report in.' His voice betrayed the sense of utter disbelief and shock he was feeling. While his companion stood beside the scene of their discovery, Moore went off at a smart trot to find the officer in charge of their 'battle' section.

In response to the report, Sergeant Ballard of the Surrey Constabulary arrived at the scene with two constables. A tarpaulin was placed over the grave-site and arrangements made for a 24-hour police guard pending further investigation the following day.

Police officers, together with Dr Keith Simpson, who was a lecturer in forensic medicine at Guy's Hospital, London, and Dr Eric Gardner, a consultant pathologist based at Weybridge Hospital, arrived at the site at first light the next morning. The doctors cautiously disinterred the remains from their light covering of sandy soil, revealing a cadaver which was a seething mass of maggots. It had not been properly buried but merely strewn with lumps of loose earth, heather roots and pieces of brushwood, and a thin layer of sandy soil, all seemingly hastily thrown together. The wind had uncovered the right arm, the flesh of which was withered from exposure. The thumb and some fingers of the right hand had been gnawed by rodents, whose teeth marks were visible even upon a cursory examination.

The body, which was lying face downwards, was clad in a green-and-white patterned dress with a lace collar, a vest, brassière and French knickers. The victim, who was female, had worn socks, not stockings. All the underclothes were in place and had not been disturbed, leading the police to discount a sexual assault; it is most unusual for a rapist –murderer to re-dress the body after such an assault.

The cadaver was a grim sight. Little remained of the victim's head but part of the scalp and some hair. The clothing was rotting; a slip which the victim had worn had decayed completely and hung in shreds from the shoulders. The shoes were missing, and the socks were in holes. Around her neck there was a scarf of the head-square or kerchief type, which was loose as though it had been worn on her head and had slipped down to her shoulders.

The body was taken to Guy's Hospital and immersed in a tank of carbolic disinfectant prior to the autopsy which was scheduled to take place later in the day. Meanwhile a search was instituted of the area surrounding the grave-site. At the site itself pieces of bone and teeth were found which eventually enabled Dr Gardner to reconstruct almost the entire skull, except for a large piece missing from the rear of the cranium. This was thought to have been the result of a powerful blow from behind with a hard object which smashed the skull and most likely caused the victim's death.

The body proved to be that of an adolescent girl of not more than twenty. Stab wounds were found, and also defensive wounds to the right forearm and hand. There were blunt traumas to the mouth area, a fractured cheek-bone, and several front teeth missing from the jaws. These, the pathologist averred, could have been caused either by blows, or from a heavy fall on to her face. Jagged wounds were found on the feet, which pointed to the body's having been dragged across rough ground at some stage. The severe damage to the skull indicated one or more blows of great violence with a heavy blunt instrument wielded by a person of great strength. Extensive fissured fractures radiated through the entire cranium. From the degree of decomposition, the stage of the life-cycle of the maggots and the degree of growth of the heather, it was estimated that the cadaver had been lying in its makeshift grave for not less than four and not more than six weeks before its discovery.

The weapon with which the girl had been stabbed proved an enigma of great interest. The nature of the wounds suggested a marlinspike or similar instrument with a hooked tip. Portions of muscle and tendon had literally been hooked out of the wounds and then torn across, causing lacerations presenting a peculiar aspect not normally seen in simple stab wounds. This appearance suggested that the withdrawal of the weapon had been impeded by reason of its hook-like shape. No such weapon could be found anywhere in the vicinity of the grave-site.

The search of the vicinity, however, produced a number of other finds. A few yards from the grave-site lay a heavy birch stake measuring 38½ inches in length and 1¾ inches thick, and which weighed 2½ pounds. Its girth of 1¾ inches tallied exactly with the size of the skull portion missing from the rear of the cranium, but as if that were not enough, some strands of human hair were found adhering to the wood which were identical with the victim's head hair.

About 350 yards from the grave-site a girl's shoe was found, and this fitted the right foot of the corpse. The left shoe was later picked up some 25 yards from the site where the right shoe was found. A canvas bag containing a piece of soap and a rosary was discovered, together with a Service water-bottle. The undergrowth also produced other items scattered over a wide area, including a green purse, some religious tokens, a New Testament, a crucifix and a small white elephant charm. These, it was considered, had once been the contents of a woman's handbag, but no such handbag was ever found. But the most important clue to the identity of the dead girl was an identity card, found together with a National Insurance card in dense bracken, bearing the name Joan Pearl Wolfe. Still later, a letter, a religious tract and an Army marriage application form were discovered, giving the name of Joan Pearl Wolfe, her date of birth – 11 March 1923 – and her place of birth. The letter was signed 'Joan' but it was not known to whom it was addressed, as it started only with the words 'My darling'. What the letter did make clear, however, was that the writer was pregnant and the addressee was a Serviceman. The writer was pressing for an early marriage on account of the coming baby.

The finding of these documents led to a swift identification of the victim. Joan Pearl Wolfe, aged nineteen, was the daughter of a widow living in Tunbridge Wells. It was soon discovered that, 2½ years previously, she had left home and became what is known as a 'camp-follower' – a girl who hangs around military camps and associates with soldiers. From time to time she had had temporary factory jobs.

The next step was to trace her known male associates, in particular the soldiers with whom she kept company. It was soon discovered that she was well-known in the area as 'the wigwam girl', who lived in a kind of wigwam or shack built from branches and twigs in the woods. This crude abode had been constructed for her by a French-Canadian soldier named August Sangret, from nearby Jasper Camp. Sangret was part Cree Indian, twenty-nine years old, and had met Joan Wolfe in Godalming on 17 July 1942, only three months before her body was found. It was common knowledge among the soldiers of Sangret's company that he and Joan had some kind of understanding that they would be married.

After this meeting in a Godalming pub, the two continued to see each other on a regular basis, and eventually Joan found that she was expecting Sangret's child. She immediately made it clear to him that he would have to marry her. When she turned up at the military camp to discuss the future, he told her that she was not allowed to stay in the camp, and it was at that point that he built for her the wigwam in the woods, roofed with his Service cape and furnished with two of his Army blankets, a tin canteen and other items. After roll-call at night, he would slip out of the camp and stay with Joan in their improvised hut, nipping back into camp in time for the morning roll-call.

About the middle of the following month Joan lost her factory job, and at the same time Sangret's nightly absences were discovered and reported to his superior officer. After a warning, he dismantled the existing wigwam and built another one about half a mile away. The next day the two of them then made door-to-door inquiries for accommodation in the nearby village of Witley, but without success. It was back to the wigwam again . . .

A few days later, on returning to camp from a route march, he was put on a charge for 'keeping a girl about the camp' and in fact Joan was in the custody of the military police. After she was released, she fainted in the street and was taken to Warren Road Hospital in Guildford, where her pregnancy was confirmed. As she was homeless the authorities agreed to keep her there until such time as accommodation could be found for her. Sangret visited her in hospital in response to a letter from her, and she asked him to take her away, which he told her he was unable to do at that time.

Early in September she again turned up at the camp, saying that she had discharged herself from hospital and that she had spent the previous night on Godalming railway station sleeping on a bench. The couple went to the village of Thursley to look for temporary lodgings, but again none was available. This time they abandoned the wigwam and slept in a disused cricket pavilion, which Sangret furnished with various Army stores he smuggled out – blankets, food, cooking utensils and so on.

A few days after they had moved into the pavilion, Sangret informed various fellow-soldiers that Joan 'had not turned up' and asked several of the men whether they had seen her. He said that he had last seen her at 6 a.m. on Monday, 14 September when he returned to camp. That same day he persuaded another soldier from his company to go with him to the disused pavilion, ostensibly to look for Joan. The man had gone with him as requested. They had seen no sign of the girl, nor any signs that she had been in the pavilion. Sangret's companion had been struck by what he consisted to be the French-Canadian's odd manner – he seemed to be acting under stress.

The following day Sangret put on a great show of searching for a lost clasp-knife. Several comrades helped him look for it. A soldier had seen such a knife stuck in a tree trunk about two months previously and recognized it as belonging to Sangret. He retrieved it and returned it to him; this was the knife that he now said he had lost.

During the weeks that followed, Sangret continued to ask his companions whether any of them had seen the girl. Eventually he told several of them, in response to their questions, that he and Joan had had an argument, and that he thought she might have gone off with another soldier who had, she told him, 'taken quite a fancy to her' and was in a better position to marry her and take her back with him to Canada. It was this man, Sangret explained, over whom they had quarrelled; he, Sangret, was the man she wanted to marry, and the child was his.

Then, on 7 October 1942, the body of Joan Pearl Wolfe was found in its lonely grave.

The Surrey Constabulary quickly called in Scotland Yard, and Chief Inspector Edward Greeno, one of the Yard's most famous detectives, was sent to head the investigation. At first sight one might have thought he would have a thankless task winkling out a suspect from more than 100,000 soldiers, based at three different camps, in the immediate area – English, Canadian and American. But Greeno's inquiries very soon elicited the fact that Joan Pearl Wolfe, a camp-follower who had associated with several different soldiers at various times, had been the current girlfriend of Private August Sangret of the Canadian Army, since this was common knowledge in Jasper Camp. It was also known that the couple had had plans to marry, and that the girl had been pressing Sangret to expedite the marriage on account of her coming child. Almost everyone in the camp knew her as 'the wigwam girl'.

Greeno wasted no time, but sought out Sangret for interview. The soldier made no secret of his association with Joan. Greeno made no mention of the finding of her body, and Sangret persisted in his story that she had most probably gone off with another soldier. Greeno told Sangret that he was investigating her disappearance. The Canadian replied that he had last seen her on the morning of 14 September, but that she had not kept a rendezvous with him for the evening at the cricket pavilion. He said that this struck him as very strange, because she had never before failed to keep an appointment with him.

After three weeks or so, he told the detective, he decided to report her disappearance to a sergeant in the military police. The soldier apparently did not know that the disappearance of a civilian should have been reported to the civil police, not the Army authorities, who had no powers in such a matter.

Greeno asked him to make a written statement – which he did, at great length – outlining his relationship with Joan Wolfe and the life they had led together living rough. He described how he built the Red-Indian-style wigwams, bending a growing sapling to the ground to make a crude frame which he thatched with heather and bracken and covered with his Army cape. He described how he snared rabbits and birds to cook over an open fire, supplemented with blackberries. Sometimes, he said, they would gather more of the profusion of blackberries than they needed, and sell them in the camp to obtain money for milk and other foods. Greeno looked at his handsome, swarthy potential murder suspect and thought he would not be out of placed as a skilled backwoodsman trained in survival tactics.

When, towards the end of his long statement, Sangret mentioned the alleged loss of his clasp-knife, Greeno wondered why he had introduced that subject. Greeno knew that the dead body of Joan Wolfe had not only been bludgeoned to death with a heavy club, but had also sustained ten stab wounds. Was the suspect concocting the story about the knife to divert suspicion from himself? Greeno was an astute and shrewd detective, conversant with the wiles of cunning suspects. He certainly thought that this kind of reasoning was behind the Canadian's story, but he did not divulge his hunch: he had no proof whatever at this stage that Sangret had killed the girl. So he ended the interview, and Sangret returned to his soldierly duties.

Meanwhile Greeno went to see Major Gray, Sangret's commanding officer, who confirmed that some time previously Sangret had asked him for an application form which a soldier contemplating marriage must fill in. The major had given him the form, which was the one, torn and dirty, that had been found in the undergrowth on the common during the police search of the area around the grave-site. The major had also met Joan Wolfe who, he said, looked as though she had been living rough, bedraggled and unkempt as she was; he had given her a pound with which to buy food and pay for lodgings. He knew that she had lived with Sangret in a wigwam, and had disciplined Sangret for not sleeping in camp. He was also aware that the girl was pregnant.

Greeno needed more proof. He obtained permission to check the suspect's kit while he was on a pay parade. One of his blankets had been recently washed, but not well enough to remove all traces of bloodstains. Still, this was not proof that he had killed anybody; the blood could quite easily have been his own. The analyst who examined the stains was unable to identify them positively as blood, much less to type them, but he thought they might well be.

This did not satisfy Greeno, who made some experiments of his own. He thought that the stains appeared where he would expect to find them if a victim about five feet four inches in height and stabbed in the same places as Joan Wolfe's body were wrapped in the blanket. This hunch proved to be correct.

Greeno interviewed Sangret again, this time telling him that the body had been found and that he was now pursuing a murder investigation, as opposed to a disappearance. He showed Sangret various items which had been found: part of a green dress, her shoes and socks, a pair of stockings and a black elastic garter, a rosary and a crucifix on a chain, a knitting pattern. Sangret positively identified all these items as having belonged to Joan Wolfe. 'I guess you found her,' he said. 'Everything points to me. I guess I shall get the blame.'

'Yes, she is dead,' Greeno replied.

'She might have killed herself,' Sangret offered.

'I don't think so,' said the detective. He did not add that a suicide would not stab herself ten times and hit herself on the back of the head with a club.

This second interview had not provided Greeno with any proof of a crime, and so he had to let Sangret go on his impending leave, but he was confident in his own mind that the soldier would return to camp and carry on normally. He knew that if Sangret were to go AWOL or desert, it would be tantamount to an admission of guilt, and he was too cunning to incriminate himself in that way. It was just a question of biding his time . . .

Just as Greeno had surmised, Sangret returned from leave and went about his normal camp routine. Then, on Monday, 27 November – seven weeks after the body had been found – Greeno received a telephone call from a Sergeant Wade at Jasper Camp which had him dashing from his office and jumping into his car. It was the breakthrough he had been praying for – but of the most unexpected nature.

Sergeant Wade ushered Greeno into an office and showed him a clasp-knife with an unusual hooked point, shaped almost like a parrot's beak. Asked where it had been found, Wade told the detective that someone had put it down the waste-pipe in the shower block, but that whoever had done so had been unaware that this pipe was blocked. Eventually, after a plumber had been unable to clear the pipe, the drainage apparatus was removed bodily and the U-bend dismantled. The clasp-knife was found wedged in the bend.

Despite the rust, the beak-like point was, Greeno knew, unquestionably the feature which distinguished this knife as being the one which had inflicted the curious stab wounds on Joan Wolfe's body. He had studied them so often that he knew every detail of their size and shape by heart, and it matched exactly. All that was now needed was to ascertain who had thrust the knife into the waste-pipe, fondly imagining that it would be flushed from sight.

It did not take long for Greeno to put two and two together. He recalled his first interview with Sangret, when he had made his first lengthy and detailed statement. This had taken some considerable time, the more so because Sangret was almost illiterate and an NCO had to write it on his behalf. During the interview, which took place in the guardroom, Sangret asked to be allowed to visit the toilet, and was given permission. The toilets were situated adjoining the shower block. He would have had ample time to hide the knife in the pipe during his absence from the guardroom to answer the call of nature.

Greeno did not, of course, merely accept the similarity between the knife and the 'hooked' wounds at its face value, but had the knife examined together with the wounds in the cadaver by Dr Simpson, who proved conclusively that the blade fitted exactly into the wounds, and that the disarranged muscles and tendons could have, and most probably were, hooked out by just such a blade.

A reconstruction of the crime was now staged, tracing the path along which various items had been found. This led them to work out that, quite near one of the wigwam sites, the girl had been attacked with the knife, most probably in a fit of passion during a quarrel; there was no evidence of premeditation. The girl had fled, terrified, down the hill-side, losing a number of items in her descent: the silver

crucifix and chain torn from her neck by the brushwood
through which she ran, her shoes coming off as she negotiated the uneven ground, her purse spilling open and
various items dropping out in her flight, until she dropped
the bag itself. Then, near the bottom of the hill, she
stumbled on to a military trip-wire laid along the side of a
stream, and fell flat on her face, smashing several front
teeth. Her murderer now came upon her and, seizing a
birch stake, dealt her a crushing blow on the back of the
head with his powerful hands lending the inert wood
superhuman strength, so that her skull was crushed in by
the blow. The stake had been found only a few feet away
from that spot. The body had then been dragged back into
the wood. Taking a blanket from the wigwam, he wrapped
the body in it, and then dragged it about a hundred yards
up to the top of the hill to the site where it was found. Had
he left it in the wood, it would have been much less likely to
be discovered; but there was a reason for dragging the body
for such a distance to the highest point in the area. The Cree
Indians in their burial rites always take a body up to the
highest point in the vicinity for interment.

Sangret was part Cree Indian . . .

*   *   *

The trial of August Sangret commenced on 24 February
1943 at Kingston Assizes, in Kingston-on-Thames County
Hall. The judge was Mr Justice Macnaghten, and the counsel for the Crown, instructed by the Director of Public
Prosecutions, were Mr Eric Neve, KC, and Mr Geoffrey
Lawrence. Sangret was defended by Mr Linton Thorp, KC,
with Mr Lawrence Vine acting as his junior.

When Sangret had been charged with the murder of Joan
Pearl Wolfe, he had replied, 'I didn't do it. Someone
did, but I'll have to take the rap.' He stood now in the
dock, facing the 'rap' he would have to take for his own
unadmitted crime, as he pleaded not guilty.

The prosecution made much of the fact that Sangret had
made some rather odd remarks to the soldier whom he had
asked to accompany him in his search for the girl. On their

way to the disused cricket pavilion, he had said, according to this soldier's evidence from the witness-box: 'I think she is crazy enough to go and kill herself if she got disgusted with life, having no proper home. If she did something to herself, I am scared that the blame would fall on me.'

Another witness, Sergeant Wade, testified that Sangret had said to him on one occasion after Joan's disappearance, 'If she should be found and anything has happened to her, I do not want to be mixed up in it.'

'You may think, members of the jury,' Mr Neve replied, 'that this was a very odd observation to make.'

However, the procession of witnesses to Sangret's remarks, odd or otherwise, did less to further the prosecution's case than the stark evidence of the injuries caused by the hook-ended knife, the knife which Sangret had professed to have lost, and had denied hiding in the shower-block drainpipe. The testimony of Dr Gardner, the pathologist, proved conclusively that the wounds in question, which had strands of muscle and tendon looped out of them, could not merely have been made by any knife or other weapon with a hook at its extremity, but that they had been made by the knife in question, the particular knife which several witnesses had sworn in testimony was the undisputed property of August Sangret. On examination, the knife (Exhibit 4) was also found to have been washed – and since the shower-block waste-pipe had been blocked and out of use for about two months previous to its employment as a hiding-place for the knife, it was bone dry and no water had passed through it. The knife had been tested for bloodstains, but these were impossible to prove conclusively as the washing had been carried out very thoroughly.

Dr Roche Lynch, official analyst to the Home Office, testified that he found a reaction from material he had scraped from the fingernail-groove on the blade, when applying the benzidine test. This reaction, he said, gave a positive result, but that test alone was insufficient to establish conclusively that blood had been present. As he said, 'All I can say is that there may have been blood there, but I cannot prove it.' The reason for this is that the benzidine test gives a positive reaction with other substances besides blood, and therefore one cannot say that blood is present simply by the use of this test. Had Dr Lynch been examining this knife today, more than forty years later, he would have had no difficulty in determining whether blood was present or not, owing to the much more sophisticated tests for the presence of blood used these days.

The defence made a valiant effort to try to exonerate the accused, even putting him in the witness-box, where he detailed at great length his association with the dead girl, his intention to marry her, his admission of liability for the child, his loss of his knife, and his denial of some of the remarks he was alleged to have made to Sergeant Wade and to the soldier with whom he had gone to look for Joan. But the evidence against him was overwhelming, both circumstantial and, above all, forensic. Few in that courtroom thought that he would not be found guilty, though a few considered that the verdict might be one of manslaughter rather than murder, committed in a jealous rage when the subject of another soldier had cropped up. It could, perhaps, be speculated that Joan may have told Sangret of this soldier's interest in her – or even invented the story altogether – purely in order to make him jealous and thus spur him into hastening the marriage which she so ardently desired and which he had every intention of entering into. Witnesses were found who averred that he had told them that the delay was simply because they could not find a settled place to live.

It was the sixth day of the trial. After the judge's summing-up, which seemed fair and unbiased, the jury, who asked and were given permission to take the skull of the dead girl and the knife labelled Exhibit 4 with them into the jury-room, were out for exactly two hours before returning with a verdict of murder, which was unanimous, but adding a strong recommendation to mercy.

On being asked whether he had anything to say as to why sentence of death should not be passed, Sangret said simply, 'No, sir. I am not guilty, sir. I never killed that girl.'

An appeal was heard on 13 April 1943, but was dismissed, and on 29 April he was hanged at Wandsworth Prison.

In a letter from Joan found in Sangret's possession after his arrest, and written to him from Warren Road Hospital in Guildford, there is the following sentence: 'We have so many things to think about and to laugh at. Do you remember the camp guards who used to watch us through their field-glasses as we walked across the fields through the heather?'

The guards would no longer be able to watch this tragic couple, and the Canadian Indian and his wife-to-be, the mother of his unborn child, would no longer be able to think of anything, nor to laugh. For she, wild and free, had been struck down by the hand of the man who, after his own fashion, had loved her, and he had gone to his account.

A SELECTION OF NOVELS AVAILABLE
FROM BANTAM BOOKS

☐	17510 6	**A Great Deliverance**	*Elizabeth George*	£3.99
☐	17606 4	**Motive To Murder**	*Georgina Lloyd*	£2.99
☐	17605 6	**One Was Not Enough**	*Georgina Lloyd*	£2.99
☐	17602 1	**Search The Shadows**	*Barbara Michaels*	£2.99
☐	17599 8	**Shattered Silk**	*Barbara Michaels*	£3.50
☐	17694 3	**Smoke and Mirrors**	*Barbara Michaels*	£3.99
☐	17204 2	**The Sicilian**	*Mario Puzo*	£4.99
☐	17524 6	**The Spy In Question**	*Tim Sebastian*	£3.99
☐	40055 X	**Spy Shadow**	*Tim Sebastian*	£3.99
☐	17697 8	**The Blooding**	*Joseph Wambaugh*	£3.99
☐	17555 6	**Echoes In The Darkness**	*Joseph Wambaugh*	£3.99
☐	40255 2	**The Golden Orange**	*Joseph Wambaugh*	£3.99

NAME (Block Letters) ....

ADDRESS ....

....